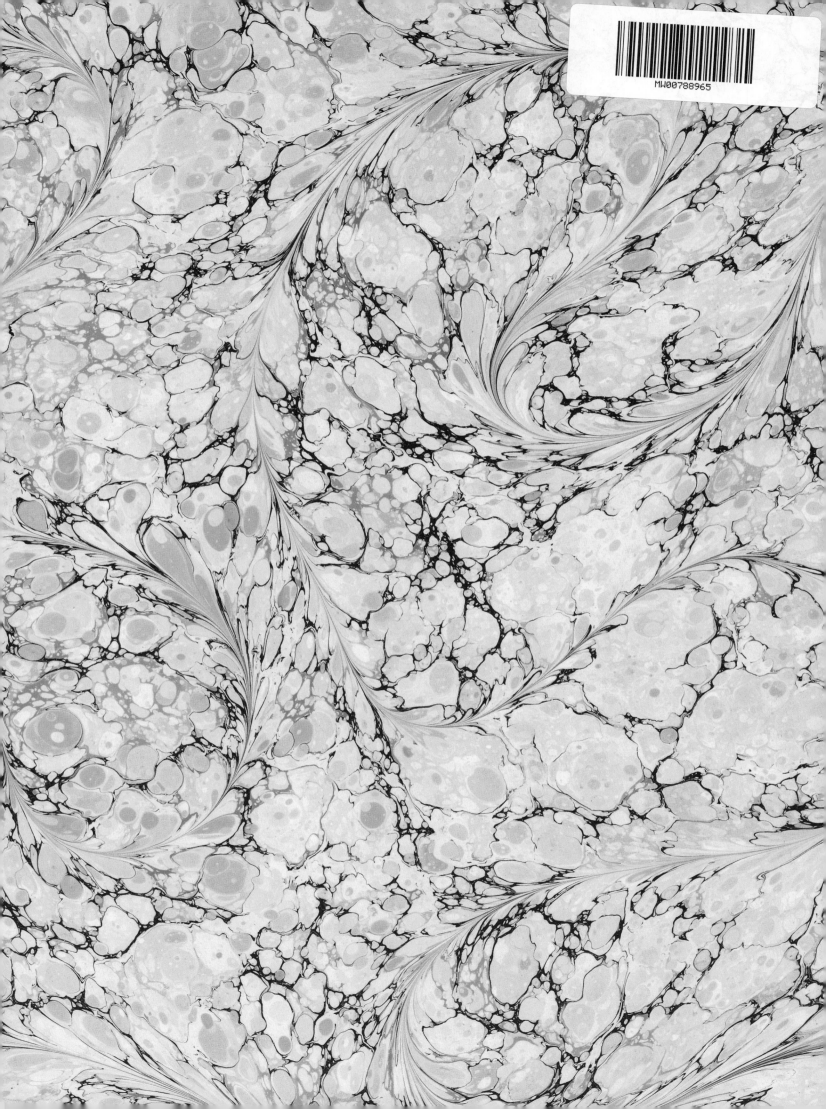

MW00788965

Victorian Staffordshire Figures 1875-1962

A. & N. Harding

Portraits

Decorative and Other Figures

Dogs and Other Animals

Later Reproductions

4880 Lower Valley Road, Atglen, PA 19310 USA

Library of Congress Cataloging-in-Publication Data

Harding, Adrian, 1942-
    Victorian Staffordshire figures, 1875-1962 / A. & N. Harding
      p. cm.
    ISBN 0-7643-1799-7 (Hardcover)
1. Staffordshire pottery--Catalogs. 2. Pottery figures,
Victorian--England--Staffordshire--Catalogs.
I. Harding, N. (Nicholas)
II. Title.
NK4087.S6H253 2003
738.8'2'094246075--dc21

                    2003005235

Copyright © 2003 by A & N Harding

All rights reserved. No part of this work may be reproduced or used in any form or by any means—graphic, electronic, or mechanical, including photocopying or information storage and retrieval systems—without written permission from the publisher.
The scanning, uploading and distribution of this book or any part thereof via the Internet or via any other means without the permission of the publisher is illegal and punishable by law. Please purchase only authorized editions and do not participate in or encourage the electronic piracy of copyrighted materials.
"Schiffer," "Schiffer Publishing Ltd. & Design," and the "Design of pen and ink well" are registered trademarks of Schiffer Publishing Ltd.

Designed by Joseph M. Riggio Jr.
Type set in Calligraph421 BT/ Garmondl TC Bk BT

ISBN: 0-7643-1799-7
Printed in China
1 2 3 4

Published by Schiffer Publishing Ltd.
4880 Lower Valley Road
Atglen, PA 19310
Phone: (610) 593-1777; Fax: (610) 593-2002
E-mail: Info@schifferbooks.com
Please visit our web site catalog at www.schifferbooks.com
We are always looking for people to write books on new and related subjects. If you have an idea for a book, please contact us at the above address.

In Europe, Schiffer books are distributed by
Bushwood Books
6 Marksbury Ave.
Kew Gardens
Surrey TW9 4JF England
Phone: 44 (0) 20 8392-8585; Fax: 44 (0) 20 8392-9876
E-mail: Bushwd@aol.com
Free postage in the U.K., Europe; air mail at cost.

This book may be purchased from the publisher. Include $3.95 for shipping.
Please try your bookstore first. You may write for a free catalog.

Contents

Acknowledgments

The authors wish to thank the many collectors and dealers who have made their figures available to us for photography, some have expressed a wish to remain anonymous, and we are happy to respect that wish. We are also happy to pay tribute to those who do not require anonymity, and in no particular order of merit we would thank, Mr. A. & Mrs. P. Wood, Mr. J. McDowell, Mr. R. Elsey, Mr. R. Walker, Mr. H. Ryans, Michael Paul Sage, Mr. & Mrs. T. Bernard, Russell Baldwin & Bright, Crows Auction Rooms, S.J. Hales, and Staffordshire Pride.

We can be contacted by mail, or in person at Tunbridge Wells Antiques, 12 Union Square, The Pantiles, Royal Tunbridge Wells, Kent, England TN4 8HE. Or you can visit our website at: **www.staffordshirefigures.com**, or e-mail us at **nick@staffordshirefigures.com**.

—A & N Harding

Introduction

From the early 1900s up until the 1950s, the collecting of Victorian Staffordshire figures was unheard of, other than by those whom people deemed as eccentrics. For a long time the realisation that they were an art form was sadly overlooked.

After the end of the Second World War, when the visiting sailors, soldiers and aircrews returned home, it was to America that thousands of these figures were taken back as mementoes of their visit to England. The exodus of figures continued when American tourists returned after the war, at which time they were very inexpensive and recognised as charming and typical of an age that has long since past.

If the British were slow to realise this forgotten art form, the situation soon changed and by the 1960's collections were being formed, a number of which have subsequently been bequeathed to, or were purchased by museums.

Victorian Staffordshire figures had finally achieved the appreciation that they so justly deserved in their own homeland.

The collecting of Victorian Staffordshire figures is now firmly established, and never again will we see them dismissed as mere 'pottery chimney pieces.' The prices now realised for the rarest and best compare to and exceed the prices paid for porcelain figures made at the same time. The prices paid for our unknown potters' work often exceeds that of marked Dresden, Meissen and other Continental factories' figures.

Books

By 1955 Mr. R. Haggar had published his book 'Staffordshire Chimney Ornaments.' This was followed in 1958 by Thomas Balston's book 'Staffordshire Portrait Figures of The Victorian Age,' this book contained for the first time, a quite comprehensive catalogue of the many different 'Portrait Figures' that had been produced.

This in turn led to increased interest in the subject, with articles appearing in magazines and smaller books on specific collecting themes being published.

This all revived interest in the forgotten art and in 1970, P.D. Gordon Pugh's book 'Staffordshire Portrait Figures of The Victorian Era' was published. It contained illustrations of over 1300 figures. 1971 saw the publication of Anthony Oliver's book 'The Victorian Staffordshire Figure' which complemented Pugh's publication and in 1981 a further book by Anthony Oliver was published 'Staffordshire Pottery the Tribal Art of England.' In 1990 Clive Mason Pope had privately published 'A – Z of Staffordshire Dogs' which for the first time catalogued subjects other than portrait figures.

In 1998 we published our two-volume work 'Victorian Staffordshire Figures 1835-1875' which contained illustrations of over 2900 figures and for the first time catalogued the entire range of figures produced in the potteries during that period, not just portraiture, but including all the decorative figures as well as, Religious, Animals, Cottages and Theatrical including Dancers and Musicians. In 2000 due to the success of the two previous volumes a further volume 'Victorian Staffordshire Figures 1835-1875 Book Three' containing over another 1100 figures was published.

This book is an attempt to conclude the cataloguing of the Victorian Staffordshire figures started in our previous books. It is also intended to bring the reader up to date with what was produced in the 87 years until production ceased in 1962.

Figures Included

As with our three previous books, this book is once again primarily a picture book containing over three hundred photographs, illustrating over four hundred figures virtually all in colour, with a potted biography of each individual portrayed and wherever possible a source or the inspiration of the figure. When we have not been able to obtain a photograph of a known portrait figure, they have been listed, described, and given a figure number.

Many of the figures produced after 1875 had also been made before that date. It has been recorded that The Parr-Kent pottery purchased a number of moulds from other potteries which had or were in the process of closing down. Parr-Kent then continued with production of these figures.

To avoid confusion, we have allocated these figures with both a new figure number, and the number it was allocated in our previous books Victorian Staffordshire Figures 1835-1875 (V.S.F.)

Prices

As with most antiques, the quality and condition of a Staffordshire figure does vary, and no two are exactly alike. The price paid for a piece will not only reflect this, but also where it was bought. The figure will likely be more expensive if it comes from a specialist who will have a large stock from which to choose, and who will offer advice and detail any repairs or restoration, rather than a market stall where the figure is part of a general stock and which the trader knows little or nothing about.

In the author's opinion auction prices are not a reliable guide; there have been any number of occasions where figures have reached prices at auction that have not been sustained and had the purchaser contacted a specialist dealer the figure could have been acquired for less.

There are a number of reasons for this situation:

- Private purchasers may not realise that they are bidding against a very high reserve.
- It only needs two bidders who are intent on acquiring the figure for the price to escalate.
- And do not forget "Auction fever" which can occur when drawn on by the occasion and a persuasive auctioneer, the buyer pays a price that is later regretted.

Guide Prices

Against each figure a **GUIDE** price is given. We must emphasise that this price is not necessarily the price for the figure shown, but for a figure in reasonable condition with little or no repairs or restoration. Within this **GUIDE** price:

- If the figure is pristine or unique, it is likely to be above the higher guide price.
- A heavily restored figure or one of poor quality or in need of repair should be below the lower guide price.
- Prices for Staffordshire figures in the United Kingdom are considerably lower than prices in the United States, so that a direct conversion is not applicable. There are exceptions to this, however. Portrait figures, whilst eagerly sought after in Britain are not so commercial in America unless they are of American personalities, and decorative figures have always been more popular and expensive in the United States.

Very few post 1875 figures at present fetch over £1000, ($1600). This situation is unlikely to continue, as the same could have been said a few years ago for pre 1875 figures, many of which now regularly reach over twice that figure.

£ Pounds Sterling		$ U.S. Dollars	
A+	Figures above £4000	A+	Figures above $8000
A	Figures £3000 to £4000	A	Figures $6000 to $8000
B	£2000 to £3000	B	$3500 to $6000
C	£1000 to £2000	C	$2000 to $3500
D	£500 to £1000	D	$1000 to $2000
E	£300 to £500	E	$600 to $1000
F	£150 to £300	F	$300 to $600
G	£50 to £150	G	$100 to $ 300
H	Below £50	H	Below $100

Buying and Selling

Very few figures from the nineteenth century have survived in pristine condition and purchasing these figures will be expensive, for when they are offered for sale they are much sought after. To be called pristine, a figure in order of importance must be:

1. **PERFECT.** No damage, restoration, repairs, chips and not stained or heavily crazed.
2. **WELL MODELLED.** Early from the mould with sharp features and details.
3. **COLOURED.** Enamels not flaked or faded.

4. **TITLED.** This applies mainly to portrait figures, for a titled figure, all other constraints applying, will always be worth more than its untitled equivalent.

It is to be accepted that the majority of Portrait figures produced after 1875 were only made in the white, they are not coloured apart from pink for the face and hands, the black for the shoes and hair, underglaze blue ceased for all intents and purposes to be used at all.

As well as the above, two other factors are most important and they are the **RARITY** and **DESIRABILITY** of the figure, when all these criteria are met record prices are paid.

Rarity and Desirability

A figure often appears to be much rarer than it actually is, this is usually because it is collected and sought after by a wider range of collectors. An example of this is the figure of Edith Cavell. Her appeal is not only to Staffordshire collectors, there are also many doctors, nurses and others in the medical profession who do not collect Staffordshire but would still buy a figure of her. Other examples are the figures of politicians, we can sell as many figures of Gladstone as we can find, usually to aspiring politicians.

True Pairs and Matched Pairs

Many Staffordshire figures were made in pairs, over the intervening period many figures have lost their original pair, this is particularly true with many of the dogs. Dealers and collectors over the years have matched singles to form **matched** or **matching pairs** often it is difficult to detect that this has occurred, and if they are a very good match the price differential between them and a 'true' pair will not be noticeable.

However we have seen **matched** pairs of dogs where one is half an inch or so smaller than the other, presented as a 'true' pair of 'dog and bitch,' this never happened, as invariably a pair is of much the same size, and if there is a detectable size differential they have been matched, and a correspondingly lower price should be paid.

Another point to remember when attempting to match a pair, is that the left hand side figure is now rarer than the right hand side counterpart, this was due to the fact that left-handedness was actively discouraged and figures picked up with the weaker hand were more likely to be dropped and damaged.

Where is the best place to purchase figures?

Specialist Dealers

We believe that although we have a vested interest, the answer is the specialist dealer.

- The specialist dealer will have a large selection to choose from, these figures may be handled and you will obtain advice and information.

- Any repairs or restoration will be pointed out to you, and many will be happy to part exchange or buy back any unwanted figures.
- You will not be sold reproductions and many will be happy to seek out particular figures for you.

Fairs and Markets

If you are looking for a bargain the best places to search are fairs or street markets. Dealers will usually arrive as the fair opens, so to obtain a bargain you must be prepared to arrive very early. There are now some major fairs where over four hundred stands are accommodated and there are usually some Staffordshire figures to be found. Care must be taken for it is at these places that either through intent or ignorance, reproductions are sold as the genuine article.

Auction Houses

Do beware, at an auction very often the condition is not stated and repair and restoration can be missed, if considering buying a figure ask the auctioneer for a condition report, although if provided it is no guarantee, so try to thoroughly examine the figure. You must realise that once the hammer has dropped it is yours, and there is no going back. Determine your price and stick to it.

In the United Kingdom estimates are usually published in the catalogue or are available in the saleroom and the lower estimate is often within one bid of the reserve price. For instance if a figure is estimated at £200 ($320) to £250 ($400), the reserve price is probably £180 ($288) and the auctioneer will not sell below this figure.

At auctions there is now also imposed the 'Buyers Premium,' and at the major houses this is now 17.5% of the price paid plus a further 17.5% on this figure for Value added tax, so a successful bid of £200 ($320), will actually cost you £241.25 ($386).

Where is the best place to sell your figures?

If you have decided to sell, either one figure or a whole collection, make up your mind whether you are going to sell to a dealer or at auction. The dealer will give you a price and pay straight away, if you decide to sell at auction make sure that you are allowed to put realistic reserves on the figures. Insist that the figures are put in a specialist sale and not in a general sale. You must be prepared to wait up to a month or more for payment and be prepared to have returned those figures that did not sell.

Repairs and Restoration

Staffordshire Figures are very breakable objects, and considering that the majority were kept on open display, and some were used as spill vases, it is not surprising that damage is commonplace. The degree of damage will affect the price; and a restored piece should cost less than a repaired one.

For the purpose of clarification:

- A **RESTORED** figure is where a piece of the figure, for instance a hand or head has gone missing and the restorer has made up a replacement.
- A **REPAIRED** figure is where a piece of the figure has broken off and been stuck back.
- Both **RESTORED** and **REPAIRED** figures may have been painted over and refired.

There are of course, degrees of repair and restoration and it would be more desirable to have a figure where only a small unimportant piece had been made up, than to have the same figure repaired which had been badly damaged and in many pieces.

Restorers and Restoration

When purchasing a figure that needs repair or restoration, a restorer needs to be found. Restorers come with all levels of ability and the authors have seen figures 're-stored' that must have looked better before the 'Restorer' started work! Make sure that before you give your figure to a restorer you see examples of their finished work.

Ideally, restoration of a figure should not take place unless the restorer has another figure from which to work, or at the very least a clear, correct photograph. On a number of occasions figures have been restored to a photograph, unfortunately the photograph itself was of an incorrectly restored figure.

What is important to remember is that the best is rarely the cheapest, it will cost just as much to have the head repaired on a £100 ($160) figure as it will on £1000 ($1600) one. At the time of writing, a relatively clean break around the neck will cost about £50 ($80) to repair. This is a substantial investment in the cheaper figure, but relatively small in the dearer one. These points should be borne in mind; otherwise you may end up with a very expensive restored figure, when a similar perfect figure could have been bought for less.

In our experience of the market there are more repaired, restored and damaged figures than there are perfect. A collector who refuses to have other than perfect specimens is likely to have a small collection, missing a large number of figures that will not come his way again.

Reproductions, Fakes, and Misattributions

More and more reproductions are appearing on the market, the most convincing are being made in the Far East and are made as the originals were made by the use of press moulds. Previously most of the reproductions were made from slip moulds, which made them lighter and less convincing.

The difference between press and slip moulds is as follows:

PRESS MOULDS – A bat of clay, like a pancake is pressed by hand into the mould, this is done usually in three parts, the front, the back and the bottom, the excess clay then trimmed off, the three parts bound together and fired. Unless the figure is a spill vase or penholder a very small hole was made in the back or bottom to allow hot air to escape in the kiln, otherwise the figure could explode.

SLIP MOULD – The mould is pre-formed and hollow, and slip, which is clay that has a consistency of cream is poured into the mould, then left to dry, the excess poured away and the remainder fired. Usually with slip moulds a large hole is left in the base of the figure to allow the hot air to escape when the figure was fired.

ASK. 'Is this a genuine figure or a reproduction?' It is surprising how many people will not lie outright, they may vacillate or even say that they do not know, but few will say it is genuine when they know that it is not. If you are dealing with someone who will, then no amount of questioning is likely to elicit the truth. From the response, you will either now be sure that it is a reproduction or you will not. If still unsure proceed to:

PLATE 1
Illustrated is an original press mould for the figure of Tom King, together with a figure produced from a similar mould.

Virtually all Staffordshire figures up to 1875 were made using the press mould method, the resulting figures were heavier than those made by the slip mould process. From 1875 more and more figures were made by the slip mould method.

In the nineteenth century lead and arsenic were regularly used in the glaze, whilst resulting in lustrous glazes it also caused the early death of the dipper, this was the man responsible for dipping the figures in the liquid glaze prior to firing. Consequently he spent most of his working life with his arms submersed in this poisonous mixture, even then this was realised, as the 'dippers' wages were commensurately higher than other workers, though his life was usually considerably shortened.

Even in the Far East today these glazes are not allowed so consequently both the colouring and glaze of the reproductions do not compare with the original.

Unfortunately they are passable imitations and have and are being passed off as genuine nineteenth century figures. Had the manufacturers of these figures marked the bottom with the factory and date this confusion could easily have been avoided.

How to determine a Reproduction

The way to tell the genuine from the reproduction is by experience; this however takes time and is therefore difficult to come by, so if in doubt about a figure we would suggest the following course of action.

PICK IT UP. Look carefully at the glaze, a lead glaze tends to be deep rich and uneven, modern glazes tend to be thin, smooth and very even. Look at the colouring, the colours on reproductions also tend to be brighter and newer looking.

If the figure has been made from a slip mould, features such as noses are smooth rather than pointed, and other features are painted on, not moulded into the figure. Finally do not be convinced it is old because the glaze is cracked, this crackerlure is very easy to reproduce, and is not necessarily a sign of age.

Fakes

Fakes in Staffordshire are rare, for the market is now cluttered with reproductions to deceive the unwary and to manufacture a fake would take a great deal of time and trouble. If the intention were to sell it for a large sum, the faker would have to fool the experts, dealers and auction houses, who usually are sufficiently knowledgeable to recognise a figure that has been tampered with.

The most common faking and the easiest to accomplish is the adding of a title to an untitled figure. This practice apart, up until 1998 the authors had only seen two faked figures. In 1998 however an unscrupulous individual recognising that spaniels with flower baskets in their mouths fetched far more than spaniels without has been applying fake flower baskets to genuine pairs of spaniels, so care should be taken when purchasing spaniels with baskets in their mouths.

Some reproductions however are now nearly 30 years old and show signs of age, and unfortunately are being passed off as genuine.

Mis-attributions

It is in the field of misattributions that the greatest care should be taken, over the years on very little or no evidence, purely decorative figures have been 'Portraiturised,' so many children with or without dogs are sold or presented as 'The Royal Children.' Many average decorative figures are said to be of actors or actresses, they may be, but it is more likely that they are not, and to pay high prices for dubious attributions is not a good investment.

If the potters titled the Queen, who would have been known to virtually all of her subjects, they would have titled actors and actresses, who would have been known to very few. With two or three exceptions, all made prior to 1875, they did not, so it must be accepted that theatrical figures are of the character and not the actor. The Parr-Kent factory produced a number of figures based on engravings from Tallis's 'Shakespeare Gallery.' These figures were all titled with the character or play, the engravings all had details of the actors or actresses portraying the parts but the figures are never, with one exception, found titled with the names of the actor or actress, they were unimportant, for it was the dramatic moment that was being captured, not the person portraying it.

The way to avoid overpaying for these figures is simple. If you wish to collect Portrait figures, only pay the premium for so doing when (a) they are titled or there is a titled equivalent or (b) there is a known incontrovertible source.

If all collectors followed these two rules, there would be no reason for the imaginative attributions being made to continue. We would urge that the figures should be judged on their quality and not their identity.

Dating of Staffordshire Figures

The precise date a Staffordshire figure was produced is often difficult to establish, with portrait figures, there is usually a point of reference which makes dating easy, for instance in the case of the military commanders, the date of the war or skirmish is known, and it follows that the figure was made at that time or shortly thereafter.

With decorative subjects it is far more difficult, many were made continuously for years, with little or no changes to the colouring, unfortunately it seems that all too often, for commercial reasons a figure is dated to '1890' when the likelihood is that it was made up to sixty years later.

The Parr-Kent factory's figures in particular are extremely difficult to date accurately, up until the 1870's the decoration was very accomplished, the base was often a combed colour of green and brown, and the brush strokes could be clearly seen, all the colours were of delicate mostly pastel shades.

In the 1880's a subtle change occurred; the same palette was used but the decoration was harder and harsher,

the greens and browns whilst still showing brush strokes were no longer as refined.

By the turn of the century a further change occurred. Now instead of decorating the figures, a coating of paint was applied, in hard blocked colours, no brush strokes can be seen and the overall effect was a deterioration of the quality. This method continued until the factory closed in 1962.

PLATE 2
A PARR FIGURE, Circa 1861, GARIBALDI standing by his horse.
The two figures illustrated are early Parr figures, compare these with Figure 4123 for a later Kent version.

Although Garibaldi visited England in 1853, the earliest this figure was made was in 1861, as the source for the figure was an engraving that appeared in the supplement to 'The Illustrated London News' of January 1861. It was a very popular figure made in two sizes, nine and fourteen and a half inches, and was continued to be produced for many years, so popular in fact that in 1867 a matching figure of Napier was made to pair it, but only in the smaller nine inch size.

Around 1900 and again in about 1920 and 1955, Kent issued price lists and in all three of these the figures of Garibaldi and Napier were included, so production of this particular Garibaldi figure had continued for at least ninety years. By 1960 when Kent published their revised 1955 booklet, both figures had ceased to appear.

The earlier Parr figures are superior to the later Kent versions, and the combing on the base and of the hair that can be seen in the above figure are superb, the orange on the jacket has been lightly and delicately applied.

PLATE 3
Parr figure Circa 1865 and Kent figure Circa 1890, GARIBALDI mounted on horseback.
Two figures illustrated, a rare sparsely coloured Parr version of 1865, and a coloured Kent version of 1890.
The source for this figure and its pair, Victor Emmanuel II, is an engraving, which appeared in The Illustrated London News of December 1860, figures of this date are extremely rare, and it would appear that when William Kent acquired the pottery in the late 1870's he decided to re-issue these two figures. They are monumental figures both 15 inches high, and on comparison with the earlier figures the changes can be detected, the colours are harsher and the darker colours blocked rather than combed, this pair continued to be in the Kent price list up to and including the 1955 list, but on the revised and last list of 1960 they have been discontinued.

History

Pottery of all types has been produced in Staffordshire for many years; it has an abundance of clay and coal, the basic materials for making and firing. Figures have been made there since the early eighteenth century; this book is however concerned only with the figures that were made from 1875.

They were simplified versions of the pre-Victorian figures which had used many hand made subsidiary parts, the Victorian figures used in the main just three moulds, a front, a back and a bottom.

Because of the extreme heat of the glost oven only two colours, cobalt blue and a derivative black could be made underglaze, by 1875 the figures had been simplified further and underglaze blue was virtually never used. But improvements in the development and application of underglaze colours meant that other colours could now be applied. In practice however few were, and this use was restricted in the main to figures of lions, cats and dogs. A brown underglaze colour in a number of shades was used as well as various shades of greys, beige and

black can be found on the figures, and is a certain guide to dating as apart from black these colours were never used before 1875.

The other colours seen on figures were added after and refired at a lower temperature, these are overglaze enamels and whilst these can be flaked, the underglaze colours cannot. The darker the enamel colour, the more likely it is to flake, overglaze black which was used much more frequently than underglaze black, is the most likely to suffer.

During the early Victorian period there were numerous pot banks in Staffordshire, employing in some cases hundreds of people, others were virtually one-man bands or small family concerns. This was a time before workers rights and effective Trade Unions, workers were employed in what amounted to slave labour conditions. Children as young as five would be working twelve hours a day, six days a week and were used for many functions, including carrying the clay, painting and decorating the figures as well as pressing the moulds.

Towards the end of the century and beyond conditions improved, and improved conditions and wages meant savings had to made in production costs, and consequent upon this was the introduction of 'bright gold' on the decoration of the figures, previously the application of the gold had been made by the 'best gold' method which had required a further firing and a burnishing to achieve the final finish. Now 'bright gold' had merely to be painted on and no further firing was necessary.

Bright gold is a hallmark of this period and is another certain way of dating a figure. Best gold has a soft gold like appearance while bright gold is much harsher more brassy in appearance, and as it was only painted on it has proved less than permanent and as the figures have been cleaned over the years in many cases the bright gold has almost disappeared.

The second modification which took place after 1875 was the introduction of glass eyes on some figures, usually dogs and other animals. These glass eyes were bought in and glued into the eye sockets, or on some figures they were fixed by a metal tie, the eyes are similar to those used on dolls and teddy bears of the period and it was from these that they were copied.

The glue used was not permanent and many have lost their original eyes, it is often difficult to detect when this has happened as replacements can be very like the originals. But if the eyes are of plastic and if clear glue has been used, it can be assured that the eyes are not original as neither was used in the nineteenth century.

Thirdly, up until 1875 many of the figures were decorated with a number of overglaze enamels, a further saving in costs was made by eliminating this process; colour was restricted to pink for the faces and black for shoes etc.

There was an exception and one pottery in particular continued to produce figures fully coloured. The Parr-Kent factory which had a history going back to the early 1850's through various owners and change of names continued until 1962 making figures long after all others had ceased, and indeed appear responsible for most if not all of the figures made after 1930.

Tastes were changing, as fashion dictated, the pace of change meant that what had been accepted by one generation was looked at with disapproval by the next. Staffordshire figures had evolved and adapted for over one hundred and fifty years but their demise was in sight, the way was open for different kinds of figures to take over the mantelpieces of England. Shaw and Copestake, a Staffordshire pottery Company of Drury and Sylvan Works Longton, had been in existence since 1901 but had never made or has never been recorded making figures, in the 1930's they brought out a whole range of animals under the SYLVAC mark, their dogs and rabbits and other figures in a number of sizes and a range of colours in a matt glaze finish were very popular and are now collected quite avidly, so much so that they are now in turn being reproduced in the far East.

The major potters, Royal Doulton, who had moved from London and Coalport who had moved from Shropshire to Staffordshire in 1926 commenced making the seemingly endless figures of ladies which continue to this day, most are given Christian names and therefore appeal to that market, but many seem to be made for a short period to increase their second hand market value.

As if to make up for lost time Royal Doulton, who did not make Victorian figures, produced and continues to produce Toby and Character jugs in their thousands, they have none of the spontaneity of Victorian Staffordshire and the colouring is rigid and each identical to its predecessor. So much so that when a figure turns up that is not identical, something as seemingly as unimportant as hair colour increases the market price of the figure considerably.

Beswick another factory from the potteries started manufacturing in 1936 although another manufacturer of this name has been recorded as manufacturing 'Staffordshire Dogs' from the 1920's this potter has been responsible for the making of a vast range of storybook figures such as 'Bunnykins' where once again something as unimportant as the colour of the jacket on 'Mr. Benjamin Bunnykins will 'transform' a £50 figure into a £250 figure.

Whilst commerciality was important in Staffordshire figures, it has now been taken to illogical extremes, where particular colours and differing back stamps purport to increase the value of figures five and ten fold.

Today the output from Staffordshire is still vast, but factory production dictates quantity rather than originality, whilst some may be hand painted, it is painting by numbers, and the figures are coated with paint, the delicate brush strokes of the Victorians are now far to labour intensive to be profitable, and we will not see their like again.

The Potter

During the early part of the nineteenth century many thousands of different figures were produced by many hundreds of different potters as the century progressed a peak of production was reached around 1860, after that date the new figures that were made reduced considerably and by 1875 new figures were rare.

Taking **Portrait** figures including naval and military as an example from 1835 to 1875, a period of forty years, around one thousand different figures were made. From 1875 to 1962, a period twice as long only around one

hundred new figures appeared, and after 1902 with the exception of The Wilkinson jugs, less than five have been recorded. With decorative figures the story is much the same, few new figures were being made and much of the production was of figures that had been produced prior. The exceptions were the continuing demand for comforter dogs of which quite a number of new figures were made as well as figures mainly in underglaze brown of standing and seated lions.

Clearly as the demand for Staffordshire figures declined so did the number of potters making them, by the turn of the century only a handful remained, by far the most important of these was William Kent. Although Sampson Smith, James Sadler, Lancaster & Sons and Joseph Unwin continued production and factory marked figures by them have been recorded but as before the majority of potters did not mark their figures and therefore they cannot be identified with a particular potter.

Parr-Kent Factory

This pottery commenced at 34 Church St. Burslem under the auspices of Mr. Thomas Parr in 1852. It continued under this name until 1870 when the name and address changed to Mr. John Parr at Wellington St. Burslem.

A Mr William Kent had been in partnership with Gaskell and Parr in Burslem and this partnership was dissolved in 1878 at that time Mr. Kent built a factory at Auckland St Burslem and traded from that date until 1894 under the name of Kent & Parr which name survived until 1894 when the pottery became William Kent and finally in 1944 it became William Kent (Porcelains) Ltd. production of figures ceased at the end of 1962.

As late as 1955 William Kent issued a coloured catalogue of their range of figures and many of these figures can be identified as having first been produced in the 1850's to 1860's. The catalogue is reproduced here in its entirety, and it is certain that a number of the figures were not originally made by The Parr Kent factory, as other potteries went out of business Parr Kent acquired the moulds and continued production.

As they have printed in their catalogue **"Kent's old Staffordshire pottery is not reproduction because except for a period during wartime the pottery has been produced continuously from the early days."**

This line of potters started at the beginning of production of Victorian Staffordshire and continued to late into the twentieth century they were amongst the first and were certainly the last to produce figures, their range was enormous, partly due to buying other potteries moulds.

When most other potteries were making "flatbacks" they had to a major extent ignored the mainstream and continued to make figures in the round, for whatever reason they were successful and continued long after their competitors had ceased. Their earlier production is superior to that made later, gradually the decoration which in the earlier figures of the 1850's and 1860's, is a delicate combing of colours particularly on the base, becomes in the 1880's and 1900's, a coating of paint in a block of colour, the modelling remains quite good throughout and it is from the palette used that the figures can best be dated.

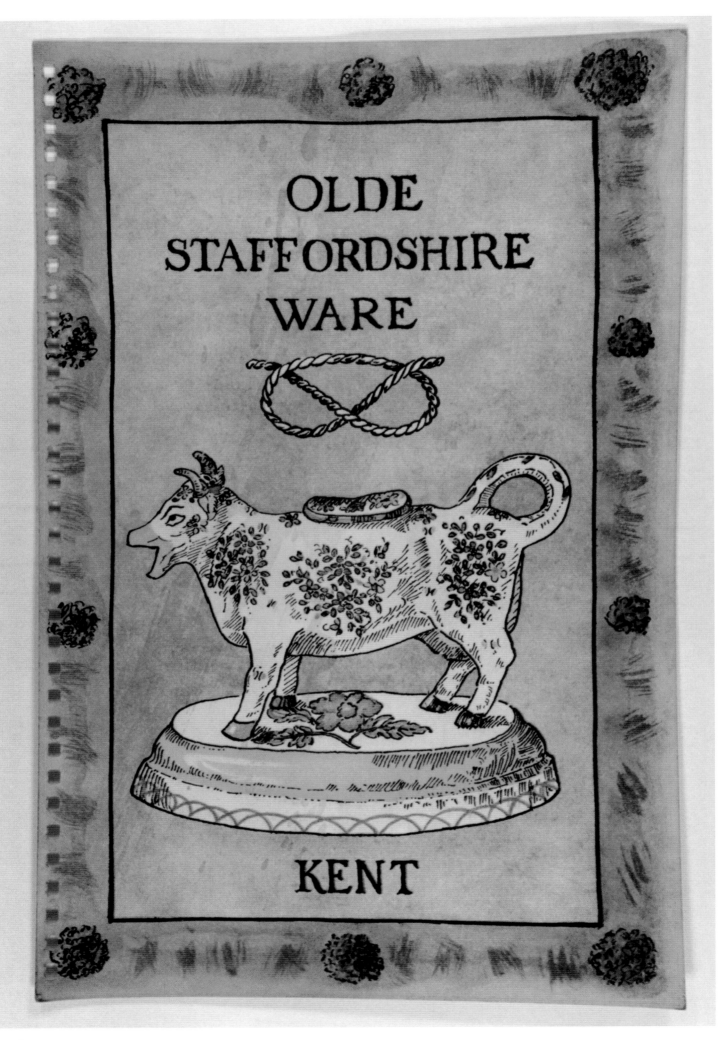

Plate 4

12

THE STORY OF
"OLD STAFFORDSHIRE"
POTTERY
BY KENT OF BURSLEM

EDITED AND ILLUSTRATED BY DOUGLAS C. HALL

1955
REVISED 1960

PRESENTED BY

WILLIAM KENT (PORCELAINS) LTD., BURSLEM

Telephone:
Stoke-on-Trent 84237/8/9

Telegrams and Cables:
Kenelec, Stoke-on-Trent

Plate 5

FOREWORD

THE PRESENT GENERATION DEDICATES THIS LITTLE BOOKLET TO THOSE MEMBERS OF THE KENT FAMILY, BOTH PAST AND PRESENT, WHO HAVE OVERCOME GREAT DIFFICULTIES THROUGH THE YEARS TO PRESERVE OUR FAMILY HERITAGE "OLD STAFFORDSHIRE POTTERY".

AND

TO OUR MANY WORLD-WIDE COLLECTOR FRIENDS WHO STILL FIND INTEREST IN PRESERVING EXAMPLES OF CRAFTSMAN-SHIP BY WHICH THE WORK OF THE INDIVIDUAL ARTIST IS EXPRESSED IN FORM AND COLOUR IN THE TRADITIONAL OLD STAFFORDSHIRE STYLE OF POTTERY.

JOHN S. KENT.

BURSLEM, 1955.

Plate 6

CRAFTSMEN AT WORK

A SECOND GENERATION CRAFTSMAN AT KENT'S

OUR YOUNGEST ARTIST

ARTISTS ALL

Plate 7

"Old Staffordshire"

IN 1878 William Kent, a potter from a family of potters, established a works in Burslem, the "Mother Town" of the potteries. Ever since then, with the exception of a short period during wartime, the Kent family firm has been producing Staffordshire pottery. In this sense, the figures which they make today can hardly be called reproductions— particularly since the moulds used are themselves produced from the original nineteenth century mastermoulds. Each piece is made by the old method of "pressing", entirely by hand from plastic clay. Once the piece has been fired it is then painted by the artists who follow the old styles, patterning and colour.

The firm have recently produced a most attractive booklet showing some examples from their wide range of pieces made from these old moulds. It is fascinating to see that such characters and traditional figures as the Watchman, the Flower Girl, the News Girl, the Crossing Sweeper, the Sailor's Farewell, and Tam O'Shanter are still being made today exactly as they were eighty years ago. These are not, of course, antiques, nor are they reproductions—they are a fine example of living tradition.

REPRINT OF ARTICLE Published in "The Antique Dealer and Collectors' Guide." July, 1958, by whose kind permission it is reproduced.

WILLIAM KENT (PORCELAINS) LTD.,
BURSLEM, STOKE-ON-TRENT, ENGLAND.

Plate 8

"OLD STAFFORDSHIRE" POTTERY
A FAMILY TRADITION :-

WILLIAM KENT, THE FOUNDER

E. J. KENT

S. H. KENT

W. F. KENT

J. S. KENT

LET CRAFTMANSHIP PREVAIL

KENT of BURSLEM, ENGLAND

Plate 9

OUR STORY

Sitting in the modern office of a highly mechanised factory (making, in the main, porcelain fittings for our great Electrical Industry), it is difficult to believe that in this same street a few generations ago stood some of the old cottages-cum-works where families made "Old Staffordshire" pottery, with the green fields as a background.

Fortunately, the Kent family has retained a small portion of the present factory wherein "Old Staffordshire" style pottery is still made from moulds produced from the original master-moulds. Craftsmen make each piece of pottery by the old method of "pressing", entirely by hand from plastic clay. After firing, each piece is decorated by brushwork which is applied by craftswomen, so that each piece carries the personal touch of the artist.

Burslem, our home town, has been rightly called "The Mother Town" of The Potteries. It was the birthplace and workshop of so many of our greatest sons of potting. Josiah Wedgwood, F.R.S., was born and worked here. He, along with other great potters of his day, rather emulated the classics in pottery, so bringing world fame to pottery formed in that manner.

Another great potter—one Ralph Wood—probably the creator of the English Toby Jug, established what could be called "Topical" Staffordshire pottery, depicting in local style, great personages, events, customs and everyday subjects in clay and colour.

William Kent, our founder, followed on somewhat similar lines to the latter. A potter, of a family of potters, he established a works in the year 1878 on the site of the present factory, and the family is still making "Old Staffordshire" pottery here.

Plate 10

18

The illustrations of this little booklet recall the story of the old times as depicted by local potters in their day :—

The donkey with panniers No. 73, seems to indicate early means of transport. A well known character about 1860 was Sally Commodore with her team of donkeys carrying Pottery from Burslem to Liverpool.

The "Coach Dog" No. 14, recalls the coaching days when Dalmation dogs sat around the old coaching Inns.

The Vicar and Clerk, No. 393, with the double-decker pulpit, a relic of those easy-going days.

"Inebriates", No. 277 and "Gin and Water" No. 258 coupled with "Willie Brewed" jugs and mugs showing the relaxation of those Old times.

Punch and Judy, Hare and Hound, Huntsman, etc., depict simple sports and pastimes of the period.

Even simple local events were portrayed by figures, or groups of figures, as in "Sailor's Farewell", "The Crossing Sweeper" and "Newsgirl" Nos. 349, 187 and 187B.

Figures, groups of figures, busts and statuettes portrayed, Worship, Royalty, Drama, Poetry, Statesmanship, The Squire, The Peasant, The Castle and The Cottage.

Conventional treatment of animals and birds in simple form along with a "Crinoline Lady" of graceful form and exquisite colouring presents a thoroughly topical collection for your delight and as a relic and lasting tribute to those "Old Staffordshire" times expressed in pottery.

Plate 11

MUG, "WILLIE BREWED", WITH FROG, Nº240.

JUG, MALT, WILLIE BREWD A PECK O' MALT. Nº304.

MUG, DOG, WITH, OR WITHOUT FROG. Nº239.

CASTLE. Nº202.

INEBRIATES Nº277.

VICAR & CLERK. Nº393.

BUST, GEORGE WASHINGTON, Nº173.

BOX, HEN & CHICKS, Nº142.

SWAN & INK Nº357.

BOX, HEN, Nº159.

VIRGIN & CHILD, Nº395.

Plate 12

HEARTY GOODFELLOW Nº 373.

SQUIRE Nº 380.

SNUFFTAKER Nº 390.

JUDY Nº 382.

ORDINARY Nº 387.

PUNCH Nº 381.

JUDY CREAM JUG Nº 315.

TOBY TEAPOT Nº 366.

PUNCH CREAM JUG Nº 315.

Plate 13

TOBY MUG,   Nº368.

WATCHMAN Nº464.

JOLLY MILLER Nº370.

SOUTER JOHNNY Nº470.

TAM O SHANTER Nº471.

PICKWICK Nº391.

FIGURE, SHOEBLACK Nº345.

JOHN BULL Nº374.

Plate 14

22

DEER HUNTERS Nº211.

FRENCH FRUIT SELLER Nº218.

SMALL TOBY,
(KNEELING,)
Nº481.

SAILORS FAREWELL Nº349.

SMALL
TOBY,(MAN)
Nº481.

SCHOOL BOY & GIRL, NESTING, Nº337.

FLOWER GIRL Nº233.

SCOTCH DANCERS Nº339.

Plate 15

FRUIT SELLER (WOMAN).
Nº 228.

CRINOLINE. Nº 165.

FRUIT SELLER (MAN).
Nº 228.

NEWS GIRL.
Nº 187.

SOLDIERS FAREWELL.
Nº 348.

CROSSING SWEEPER.
Nº 187.

Plate 16

24

DOUBLE DOG (ROUGH).
Nº 15.

JUG,
KINGFISHER Nº 516.

SHEEP & RAM.
Nº 107.

CURLY DOG Nº 1.

NOVELTY FIGURE (GIN & WATER).
DOUBLE-SIDED, Nº 258.

POODLE, ROUGH.
Nº 25.

TOY HOUND, LYING Nº 79.

FACE MUG
Nº 511.

HOUND INK, Nº 82.

GIRL WITH LAMB Nº 456

TOY HOUND,
SITTING, Nº 80.

CAT ON CUSHION Nº 67

Plate 17

COW & MILKMAID (PAIR) Nº 62.

PRINCE & PRINCESS (PAIR) Nº 316.

THE PRINCE

DONKEY Nº 73.

HOUND & HARE (PAIR) Nº 85.

SPANIEL, SITTING, (PR.) Nº 32.

ZEBRA, (PAIR) Nº 113.

COW CREAM (NO STAND), Nº 60.

PARROT (PAIR) Nº 102.

VINTAGE REAPER (PAIR) Nº 394.

COACH DOG, SITTING, (Pr) Nº 14.

Plate 18

26

LARGE FLOWERED No194.

CAMPBELL COTTAGE No189.

BANK COTTAGE No178.

CHATEAU No198.

PAGODA No199.

ROUND No197.

SMALL FLOWERED No195.

THATCHED No192.

COTTAGE No505.

MAN COTTAGE No450.

SHAKESPEARE SAVING BANK

SHAKESPEARE No196.

A SELECTION FROM OUR RANGE
OF OLD STAFFORDSHIRE COTTAGES,

WILLIAM KENT LTD, BURSLEM, STAFFORDSHIRE.

Plate 19

LIST OF POTTERY MADE BY KENTS

Ref. No.		Approx. Ht. in inches	Ref. No.		Approx. Ht. in inches
115	Arab	7¼		Cow Creams on Stand—	
116	Arab Water Carrier	9¼	58	No. 1	6
541	Ash Tray, Poodle	4½	59	No. 2	5
542	„ „ Spaniel	4½	60	No Stand	4
118	Birdnesting	7¼		Cow & Milkmaid—	
120	Buttercup	11¾	61	Maid Sitting	6¼
121	Burns & Mary	12	62	Maid Standing No. 1	9¾
122	Bacchus on Barrel	6½	63	„ „ No. 2	8
128	Baby in Cradle	1¾	64	„ „ No. 3	6¼
133	Bulls Head Cheese Stand	7	65	„ „ No. 4	5¾
134	Bouquet Holder	11½	66	Cat, Standing, Wild	5
135	Bird Catcher	10¾		Cat, Sitting on Cushion—	
137	Ball Players	6	67	„ „ „ Large	7
139	Boy on Zebras	7½		„ „ „ Middle	
141	Boxes, Duck	7	501	„ „ „ Small	3¾
142	„ Hen & Chickens, large	9½	68	Camel Rider	5¼
143	„ „ „ small	6	69	Camel	6¼
159	„ Hen, No. 1	9¾	180	Children & Goat	7
160	„ „ No. 2	8¼	181	„ „ Fawn	6¾
161	„ „ No. 3	6	182	„ „ Dog	5½
162	„ „ No. 4	4½	184	Cupid Fruitsellers	9
163	„ „ No. 5	3¾	186	Christ at Well (small)	5½
	„ Pea Hen	6½	187	Crossing Sweeper & Newsgirl	7½
	„ Pigeon	5½	178	Cottages—Bank No. 1	5
165	„ Crinoline	8½	179	„ „ No. 2	4
166	„ Queen	7¼	188	„ New	5
167	Busts, Madonna	14½	189	„ Campbell (large)	8¾
168	„ Homer	12¾	190	„ „ (small)	5¼
169	„ Plato	14	191	„ Ordinary	6¾
170	„ Wesley	11½	192	„ Thatched	2¼
171	„ Alexander	10½	193	„ Oriel	4½
172	„ Locke	7	194	„ Flowered (large)	4½
173	„ Washington	8¼	195	„ „ (small)	4¼
174	„ Shakespeare	8¾	196	„ Shakespeare	4½
175	„ Britannia	14	197	„ Round	4
	Bullbaiting	5¼	198	„ Chateau	3¾
270	Columbine	7	199	„ Pagoda	6¼
54	Cow & Calf No. 1	6¾	450	„ Men	4¾
55	„ „ No. 2	6¼	474	„ Snow	5
56	„ „ No. 3	4¾	503	„ John Knox	5
57	„ „ No. 4	4¼	504	„ Shakespeare No. 2	4½

Plate 20

Ref. No.		Approx. Ht. in inches	Ref. No.		Approx. Ht. in inches
505	Cottages—Small	3¼	20	Dog, Newfoundland No. 1	9¾
521	„ Ann Hathaway's	4¼	21	„ „ No. 2	4¾
540	„ Old Curiosity		22	„ „ with Boy	9
	Shop ...	4	23	„ Prince Charles	
200	Castle, No. 1	13½		(on Cushion)	7
201	„ No. 2	10¾	24	„ Pug No. 2	5¼
202	„ No. 3	8½	25	„ Poodle No. 1 ...	10½
202A	„ Small	4	26	„ „ No. 2	9¼
203	Centrepiece, Bird & Nest	10	27	„ „ No. 3 ...	8½
204	„ Fox & Goose	9	28	„ „ No. 4 ...	7
205	„ Hound & Goat	10¾	29	„ „ No. 5 ...	6½
206	„ Scotch Coursers	10¾	30	„ „ No. 6 ...	4½
207	„ Water Carrier	10	486	„ „ Min. ...	3
208	„ Farmyard ...	10	555	„ „ on Blue Base	3½
525	Caddie (Pair to Golfer) ...	7	544	„ „ No. 6 on Base	5½
71	Deer & Fawn	8¼	31	„ Bull Sitting ...	7
522	Dog—Poodle (Standing)		32	„ Spaniel No. 1 ...	10
	with Basket	3¾	33	„ „ No. 2 ...	7¾
1	Dog, Curly No. ¼ ...	15	34	„ „ No. 3 ...	6
2	„ „ No. ⅓ ...	13½	500	„ „ Min. ...	2¾
3	„ „ No. ½ ...	11¾	554	„ „ on Blue Base	3¼
4	„ „ No. 1 ...	10½	48	„ Blenheim, Spaniel	
5	„ „ No. 1½ ...	9½		Sitting	6
6	„ „ No. 2 ...	8½	49	„ St. Bernard Standing	6
7	„ „ No. 2½ ...	7¾	50	„ Terrier No. 1 ...	8½
8	„ „ No. 3 ...	7¼	51	„ „ No. 2 ...	6
16	„ "L" No. 1 ...	10	52	„ With Bird, on Stand	4¼
17	„ "L" No. 4 ...	5½	53	„ only, on Stand ...	4¼
9	„ Collie No. 1 ...	11	52A	„ No Bird on Cushion	
10	„ „ No. 2 ...	8½		(large)	4½
11	„ „ No. 3 ...	7	52B	„ No Bird on Cushion	
12	„ „ No. 4 ...	5½		(small)	3
13	„ Coach Standing ...	6¼	546	„ Poodle Standing (small)	2½
14	„ „ Sitting ...	5	547	„ Poodle Standing (large)	3¾
15	„ Double, Rough ...	5½	523	„ Under Tree (small) ...	4
18	„ Maltese, on Stand ...	6½	535	„ Poodle Sitting	
19	„ „ No Stand ...	5½		with Basket No. 1	10½
532	„ Dalmation No. 1 ...	8½	536	„ „ „ No. 3	8½
533	„ „ No. 2 ...	6½	537	„ „ „ No. 4	7
534	„ „ No. 3 ...	4½	538	„ „ „ No. 5	6½
543	„ „ on Base ...	5½	539	„ „ „ No. 6	4½
			209	Dove Figures	6

Plate 21

Ref. No.		Approx. Ht. in inches	Ref. No.		Approx. Ht. in inches
210	Don Quixote … …	9½	524	Face, Mug (special) …	5¾
72	Donkey No. 1 … …	9¼	511	,, Frog Mug … …	4¾
73	,, No. 2 … …	7	416	Fisherman Tobacco Jar …	5½
211	Deer Hunters … …	7¼	253	Goat & Child … …	6
75	Elephant No. 1 … …	5	256	Girl & Boy Flower Gatherer	6
76	,, No. 2 … …	4½	257	Gardener … … …	7¼
77	,, No. 3 … …	4	258	Gin & Water … …	8½
78	,, and Young …	5¼	263	Garibaldi & Horse …	15
214	Emir Pasha on Horse …	4½	412	Giraffe (large) … …	7¾
215	Falstaff (large) …	9½	413	,, (small) … …	5½
216	,, (small) …	6¾	456	Girl and Lamb (paired with)	
218	French Fruit Sellers …	7¼	457	Boy and Dog) … …	5¾
220	Face Money Box (large) …	3½	525	Golfer … … …	7
220A	,, ,, ,, (medium)	3	508	,, & Caddie …	7
221	,, ,, ,, (small) …	2½	256	Grape Dancers … …	9¼
222	Fidelity … … …	5¼	526	Hound Head Stirrup Cup	4½
530	Figure Colleen … …	6	79	,, Toy, Lying …	2½
531	,, Flora … …	6	80	,, ,, Sitting …	4
259	,, Gladstone … …	11½	81	,, Leveret … …	1½
419	,, Snufftaker (small)	5½	82	,, & Ink No. 1 …	6
223	Fox Head, Stirrup Cup (large)	5	83	,, ,, ,, No. 2 …	3¾
224	,, ,, ,, (medium)	5	84	,, Sitting (small) …	7¾
225	,, ,, ,, (Vine)	4¾	85	,, and Hare No. 1	
226	,, ,, ,, (Tallio)	3½		(Hare in Mouth) …	11
227	Fruit Sellers (large) …	7	86	,, and Hare No. 2	
228	,, ,, (small) …	4¾		(Hare in Mouth) …	7¾
229	French Fiddlers (large) …	7¾	87	,, and Hare No. 3	
230	,, ,, (small) …	4¾		(Hare in Mouth) …	6
231	,, Kiss … …	9	88	,, and Hare (large)	
233	Flower Girl … …	7¼		(Hare on Stand) …	9½
234	Fisher & Bride … …	13½	89	,, and Hare (small)	
235	Fish Dealer (large) …	8		(Hare on Stand) …	6¾
236	,, ,, (small) …	7¼	90	,, and Hare Lying (large)	5¾
239	Frog Mug, Dog … …	6	91	,, ,, ,, Sitting ,,	15½
240	,, ,, Willie Brewed	6	92	,, ,, ,, ,, (small)	8¼
240A	,, ,, John Mytton	6	93	Horseman No. 1 … …	14½
241	Flower Horn, Cow & Calf	11½	94	,, No. 2 … …	9¼
242	,, ,, Donkey …	6½	95	Horse on Stand (large) …	9¼
243	,, ,, Elephant …	5	267	Highland Fling … …	8
244	,, ,, Farmyard	11	269	Happy as a King … …	7
246	,, ,, Hunter …	12	270	Harlequin & Columbine …	7
248	,, ,, Sportsman	12	271	Haymakers … …	7¾

Plate 22

Ref. No.		Approx. Ht. in inches
273	Hamlet (large)	10¾
274	,, (small)	6¾
276	Huzzar on Horse	10½
277	Inebriates	8¾
278	Infant Bacchus ...	9
461	Infantry Man	7½
96	Jockeys	7
280	Jobson & Nell (large) ...	12¼
281	,, ,, ,, (small) ...	6
304	Jug, Malt, Willie Brewed	9¾
516	,, Kingfisher	9½
527	,, Sportsman	7¾
517	,, Nelson & Hardy ...	6¼
518	,, Romulus & Remus ...	6
97	Kitten, Standing	5
100	Lion, Standing	9½
101	,, Lying	9¼
285	Love at Sight (large) ...	8
286	,, ,, ,, (small) ...	4¾
287	Lovers Gift	5½
288	,, Presentation ...	5
293	Lookers and Seekers ...	7½
294	Market Goat	7½
297	Mother Goose	7¼
299	Maternal Instruction No. 1	8
300	,, ,, No. 2	7
301	,, ,, No. 3	6
302	Macbeth	8¼
303	,, Lady	8
187	News Girl	7½
307	Organ Grinder	7
308	Ophelia	6¼
102	Parrots	7
103	Parroquets on Stump ...	9
310	Polish Farewell (large) ...	8¼
311	,, ,, (small) ...	7½
312	Peppers (Publican & Policeman)	5¼
313	Playmates	5
314	Paul & Virginia	11¾
315	Punch & Judy, Cream Jugs	4¾
316	Prince & Princess on Horse	7¾
317	Poulterers	7
321	Returning from and going to Market	7
323	Red Riding Hood No. 1 ...	15
324	,, ,, ,, No. 2 ...	7¾
325	,, ,, ,, No. 3 ...	5¾
326	,, ,, ,, No. 4 ...	4
328	Rebecca at Well (small) ...	8½
329	Romeo & Juliet	10½
104	Stag under Trees	5¼
105	Stag	11
106	Squirrel	6
107	Sheep & Ram No. 1 ...	7½
108	,, ,, ,, No. 2 ...	5
502	,, ,, ,, Miniature	3½
109	Sheep under Tree (Rough)	5
110	,, ,, ,, (Smooth)	5
330	St. Sebastian	10
332	Sweet Sixteen	4¾
334	Swiss Pets	9
337	School Boy & Girl Nesting	7½
338	Scuffle for a Nest	6
339	Scotch Dancers	9
342	Scotch Pets	6¾
345	Shoeblack	11
346	Scotch Ponies	8¾
347	Sancho Panza	7¼
348	Soldiers Farewell	8¼
349	Sailors ,, ...	10¾
528	Sportsman & Dog ...	7
355	Shylock (large)	9¾
356	,, (small) ...	7
357	Swan & Ink	3¼
507	Tythe Group No. 1 ...	5½
509	,, ,, No. 2 ...	6
506	Tenderness	7
358	Truants	7½
360	Turkish Sentinel	9¼
453	Travelling Tailor on Goat (Pair)	5¼

Plate 23

Ref. No.			Approx. Ht. in inches		Ref. No.				Approx. Ht. in inches
	Tobacco Figures—				391	Toby Jugs, Pickwick			7½
362	Buccaneer		12¼		464	„	„	Watchman	8¾
363	Snufftaker, Male		12½		465	„	„	Sailor	11
364	„	Female	12½		470	„	„	Souter Johnnie	9
366	Toby Teapots		7¼		471	„	„	Tam O' Shanter	9
367	„ Creams		3½		481	„	„	Men (small)	3¾
368	„ Mugs		5¾		481	„	„	Women (small)	3¾
369	„ Cruets		5½		481	„	„	Kneeling (small)	3½
370	„ Jugs, Jolly Miller		9		483	„	„	Men (min.)	3
371	„ „ Mermaid Handle		10		483	„	„	Women (min.)	3
372	„ „ Nelson		11½		393	Vicar & Clerk			9½
373	„ „ H. G. Fellow		11¼		394	Vintage Reaper			7¾
374	„ „ John Bull (large)		11		395	Virgin & Child			14
375	„ „ „ „ (small)		10		111	Wild Horse			8¼
380	„ „ Squire		11		400	Water Carrier			
381	„ „ Punch		12			Dog & Lamb (small)			9¼
382	„ „ Judy		11		401	Watercress (large)			9¼
383	„ „ Falstaff		8½		402	„ (small)			7
384	„ „ Cromwell		9¾		403	Wesley Figure (large)			8
385	„ „ Large		10		404	„ „ (small)			7
386	„ „ Small		9		411	Watch Stand, Youth & Age			10½
387	„ „ Ordinary		10½		112	Zebra (large)			7¾
389	„ „ Jug & Glass		9½		113	„ (small)			4¼
390	„ „ Snufftaker		8¼		541	Puppy, Begging			3½
529	„ „ A Broth of a Bhoy		7¾		542	„ Sitting			3½
376	„ „ Darby		10			Marriage Group			6
377	„ „ Joan		9			Piggybanks			2¾
378	„ „ Father Christmas (large)		8		545	Hunter & Dog			9½

The list of articles, although comprehensive, cannot be finalised as further old moulds are continually being discovered from our stock of ancient moulds. Nor can we guarantee to be able to make all the pieces listed. These are of interest to collectors — Our agents will be pleased to answer enquiries.

Plate 24

KENTS "OLD STAFFORDSHIRE" POTTERY IS NOT "REPRODUCTION" IN THE STRICTEST SENSE OF THE WORD, BECAUSE, EXCEPT FOR A PERIOD DURING WARTIME, THE POTTERY HAS BEEN PRODUCED CONTINUOUSLY FROM THE EARLY DAYS.

WE, WHO APPRECIATE THESE EXAMPLES OF A PERIOD IN STAFFORDSHIRE POTTERY HAVE TO THANK MEMBERS OF THE KENT FAMILY FOR PRESERVING THE MANUFACTURE OF TRADITIONAL POTTERY AT THE EXPENSE OF MODERN DEVELOPMENT.

THE AUTHOR—1955.

SEE LIST AT END OF BOOKLET.

WILLIAM KENT (Porcelains) LTD.,

AUCKLAND STREET,

BURSLEM, ENGLAND.

Plate 25

Plate 26

The Kent Catalogue

On examination of the booklet it can be confirmed that figures first produced in the 1850's were still being made in 1955, immediately above the head of the craftsman in the picture of 'Craftsmen at work' and at the far end of the top shelf in 'Artists all' the figures of The Prince and Princess of Wales standing before St. Bernard dogs can be seen, he as yet unglazed, she in full colour. In our book 'Victorian Staffordshire Figures 1835-1875' the same figures can be found illustrated as Figures 602/603.

To the left of the figure of The Prince in 'Craftsmen at work' a small decorative figure of a boy sitting on a fence holding his hat in the air is illustrated, this figure is also illustrated in our book (V.S.F.) **(See figure 3333A)** and can be identified as 'Happy as a King' and was first made in 1869, its source was a painting by William Collins R.A. which was exhibited at The Royal Academy in 1836.

The Kent factory in the 1950's were still making over three hundred and fifty different figures, many of these can be identified as having first been made in the 1850's to 1870's, and the description of many of those listed but not illustrated in the booklet also fit the description of figures that were first made then

In Chapter Two, a number of the figures line drawn in the booklet are illustrated and are cross-referenced to the stock number in the booklet. Many Kent figures that were made in the 1940's and 1950's have now acquired fifty to

sixty years of age and are very often now described as 'late nineteenth century.' Care should be taken as most are mid-twentieth century figures. Very few portrait figures continued to be reproduced as with the passing of time the celebrity value was lost and they ceased to be a commercial proposition.

Sampson Smith

Sampson Smith was born in 1813 and died in 1878; in 1846 he is recorded as a pottery decorator. It is not known conclusively when his pottery first started, but a number of figures have been recorded with a mark of either "Sampson Smith 1851 Longton" or "S Smith Longton 1851." These were not the date of the figures so it could be safely assumed that the pottery had put the date of its inception on the figures.

Until 1859 he was making these figures at The Garfield Pottery, High St., Longton and from 1859 until his death at The Sutherland Pottery. The business continued after his death by his executors in 1888. The business was then acquired by Adderley & Tams and in 1912 by John Adderley and W. H. Davies, in 1918 Barker Brothers were the owners and by 1954 it was part of the Alfred Clough group, there is no evidence as to when exactly they stopped producing figures but it is likely that it was around 1930.

What makes this pottery important is that in 1948 in a dis-used part of the factory about sixty old press moulds were discovered in good condition. This discovery enabled the attribution of not only the moulds found but of many other figures that were recorded and were clearly by the same modeller.

This factory was responsible for by far the greater number of new portrait figures produced after 1875, including figures of Gladstone, Beaconsfield, Sir Garnet Wolseley, The Duke of Connaught, Sir Herbert Stewart, Colonel Burnaby and The Boer War commanders General Buller, Lord Kitchener, Major Macdonald, Lord Dundonald, Lord Roberts and General French, Baden-Powell and General De Wet.

James Sadler & Sons Ltd.

This factory situated at the Wellington and Central Potteries, Burslem, only commenced production in 1899, and two figures made in the slip mould method have been recorded of Lord Kitchener and General French **(See figures 4088/4063)** marked SADLER/BURSLEM/ENGLAND. These particular figures are also found made by the more usual press mould method, and it is probable that they were made by Lancaster. Also illustrated **(See figures 4471/4472)**, a large pair of white and gilt dogs and **(See figures 4655/4656)** a pair of underglaze brown standing lions, both of which are marked SADLER/BURSLEM/ENGLAND. Up until the discovery of these marks both of these pairs of figures have been dated to the 1880's; however, as the pottery did not commence operations until 1899 it is clear that these figures are later, i.e. early twentieth century.

Lancaster & Sons Ltd.

This factory situated at the Dresden Works, Hanley also commenced in 1899, and two pairs of figures of King Edward VII and Queen Alexandra, one a pair of standing figures, the other of them on horseback **(See figures 4003/4004)** were made in the press mould method, and have been recorded bearing the marks 'Copyright Dec. 20 1901 T.H. Sandland' and 'Copyright Dec. 10 1901' on the backs of the figures

Thomas Henry Sandland joined the firm of Lancaster & Sons in 1899 and eventually became the Chairman and Managing Director of the Company. In 1944 the Company's name was changed to Lancaster & Sandland Ltd. Mr. Sandland died in 1956, being the last surviving member of the original board of directors.

It is probable, due to the similarity of the figures of King Edward VII and Queen Alexandra, that the press mould versions of the series of six figures, Sir Redvers Buller, Lord Kitchener, Hector McDonald, Baden Powell, General French and Lord Roberts, were produced by this factory, although it is certain that the slip moulded versions were made by Sadler.

Joseph Unwin & Co.

This pottery started in 1871 under the name of Poole & Unwin at Cornhill Works, Longton; in 1877 it changed its name to Joseph Unwin & Co. A figure of two harvesters has been recorded which bears the marks of this pottery, one example bears the mark 'Unwin' in a diamond motif on the back of the figure. The other the initials 'P & U' are inscribed on the base, as this figure was made for a period which saw the change of name, i.e. at least a year or so, it is therefore unlikely that this was the only figure produced, but to date no others have come to light with this factory's mark.

Arthur J. Wilkinson Ltd.

This Company was responsible for producing initially eleven character jugs of First World War notables, designed by Sir. F. Carruthers Gould, all in limited editions, (A twelfth of Winston Churchill was added in 1941). Founded in 1880 by Arthur J. Wilkinson, their trade mark was 'Royal Staffordshire Pottery,' they continued in operation for many years and their most famous designer was Clarice Cliffe who became the Art Director and whose work is now avidly collected. (She was responsible for the design of the Churchill character jug.) Amongst the other artists and designers who worked for this company were Dame Laura Knight, Sir Frank Brangwyn, Dod Proctor (all three were or became Royal Academicians), Paul Nash and Ben Nicholson.

These figures marked a change in the method and design of Staffordshire Portrait figures, as jugs and slip moulds they were unlike anything that had been produced before, they were of a very high quality and as stated made in a limited edition, each with its own certificate numbering, and authenticating the figure, as well as the base of the figures being clearly marked with designer, manufacturer and even retailer.

These jugs were probably the inspiration for Royal Doulton who have subsequently produced character jugs in their thousands, their first recorded character jug was of Charlie Chaplin and that was made in 1918

PLATE 27
The bottom of a Carruthers Gould Jug, signed and detailing the maker and retailer.

What Was Potted?

The subjects chosen by the potters were as varied as the times in which they lived. The area in which they were produced was geographically quite small, seven villages that had one thing in common, an abundant supply of coal to fuel the kilns and a more than sufficient reserve of clay to make the figures. These villages eventually grew into towns and finally into the County Borough of Stoke on Trent.

These villages were Stoke, Fenton, Longton, Tunstall, Burslem, Hanley and Shelton. Thirty odd square miles, which have over the centuries produced countless millions of pieces of pottery, not just figures, but every conceivable item from candlesnuffers to lavatory pans, jardinières, to dinner plates. It is likely that even today every home in Great Britain possesses at least one article of domestic ware that has been made in the Potteries.

Seconds

With present day production it needs a very careful eye to detect any difference between seconds and perfect examples, as methods have improved to the degree that apart from decoration, one figure is very like another, This was not so in the Victorian period, each figure made deteriorated the mould, was less sharp and had less detail than the one that went before, until a stage was reached when the moulds were scrapped and replaced by fresh ones. This continued *ad infinitum* or at least until the market for that particular figure was exhausted.

Figures can be found which have small pieces missing but glazed over which indicates that the piece was missing prior to firing, figures can also be found that have a black or yellow line on the base as opposed to the usual gilt line, careful examination of these figures will often reveal damage that occurred at the pottery usually in the kiln. These figures were no doubt sold as seconds at a lower price, and today they will fetch a lower price than their perfect counterparts.

Commercialism

It is important to remember that all the figures were produced commercially. This was the sole overriding reason for their production. All other considerations were secondary. Each and every pottery to survive had to be profitable, artistic merit was hardly contemplated. Above and beyond every other consideration the figure had to sell, a number of figures produced did not sell; today that would make them rare, if they are of quality, as well as being rare, and they are now highly regarded and consequently will be expensive.

It was commercial pressure that made the figures simple, only three part moulds meant that more could be produced for less, as the figure was to be viewed from the front, there was no need to model or decorate the back.

Thus commercialism brought about the simplicity of design that makes the figures what they are, a naive folk art. They were produced by the working class for whoever would buy them; they were hand made, yet they were part of the Industrial Revolution, using production line methods. They were displayed in the cottages and houses of the cities, towns and villages of Britain, and were exported to the Colonies, bringing life and colour to many a Victorian mantelpiece.

This was an age before radio and television, before photography was widely available. An age where illiteracy was common, people wanted heroes, nostalgia and romance. The Staffordshire figure fulfilled these wants.

Royalty

Intensely patriotic, the Royal Family was held in high esteem and virtually everyone was a Royalist. During the early part of her reign, figures of Queen Victoria and her Consort Albert were made with great frequency, as were figures of her children from babies to adults and in particular the weddings of the Prince and Princesses. By the 1870's interest had waned and only one new figure, a bust, can be said with certainty to have been made during the last twenty years of her reign, although a figure first made in 1870 was adapted for her jubilees and death.

A number of figures were made of King Edward VII and Queen Alexandra on their succession to the throne in 1901, and a figure of the ill fated Duke of Clarence (the eldest son of King Edward VII and heir to the throne) together with a figure of his intended wife Princess May (Mary of Teck) was made in 1891, but as he died before his wedding in 1892. These are very rare figures, the potters ever resourceful, adapted his figure into a portrait of Baden-Powell.

The Duke's intended spouse, Mary of Teck recovered from her grief quite quickly to marry his brother the future King George V in 1893 (of whom a character jug was made by Wilkinson Ltd.) so she became Queen of England after all.

The Russian War scare in 1877 provoked the production of figures of the principal opponents, Alexander II Tsar of Russia and Abdul Hamid II Sultan of Turkey, and these rate as amongst the finest of the late portrait figures produced.

In 1873 the Shah of Persia, Nasred-Din visited England. Subsequently a song sung by the Great Vance titled 'Have You Seen the Shah' became popular both as a song and a catchword. Three figures were modelled of him, probably in mirror image pairs, it is not certain whether they were made as a result of his visit, or due to the popularity of the song. As they are titled 'Have you seen the Shah, it was more likely that the song was responsible, whilst they could have been made before 1875 they were produced after this date and so are included in this book.

Other Portraits

In the main from 1875 it was from the military commanders of the various wars and skirmishes that the potters produced new portrait figures. In 1885 the campaign to relieve Gordon in Khartoum was commemorated with portraits of Wolseley and Gordon, in 1898 The battle of Omdurman produced figures of Kitchener and Macdonald and during the Boer War of 1899 to 1902 figures of French, Roberts, Baden-Powell, Buller, Dundonald, Kitchener, Macdonald and De Wet were made.

A figure was made of Edith Cavell, a nurse, who was court-marshalled, condemned to death, and shot by the Germans in October 1915. A series of eleven character jugs were made shortly after the war in 1918, all of First World War notables, it was rounded up to an even dozen, when in 1941 a figure of Churchill was made.

Figures of politicians in this period were made of the Prime Ministers Disraeli and Gladstone as well as the Member of Parliament, Thomas Sexton.

The Workers

Many people had left the land to work in the ever increasing factories of the towns, and cities and what better to remind them of what they had left behind, than a figure of rural life. No aspect escaped their attention, farmers, farmhands, milkmaids, milkmen, poachers, hunters, shepherds and of course the farm animals they attended, sheep, cows, goats, rabbits, no pastime, recreation, pursuit, craft, or occupation was forgotten. It is here, amongst these decorative figures that the potters were able to indulge their whims and fancies, and produce some of the finest examples of their art, though by the late 1870's fewer and fewer new figures were being made, most of the potters relying on models that had first been produced years before.

Circus/Theatre

On high days and holidays, the circus came to town, and with it the side shows and catchpenny booths, the fortune teller, the tightrope artist, the lion tamer and clowns, it is not known for certain but it is more than probable that all these figures and more would have been sold there. Attendant upon the fairs and circuses were the travelling people, the gypsies, who adroit at turning a few words into a few coins, would tell the fortunes of the impressionable visitors to these glamorous places.

At the time not only was the theatre in its heyday, but Astley's, a cross between theatre and circus, was enjoying enormous popularity. Here was to be found melodrama at its height, and almost everything was produced, even Shakespeare on horseback. It was here that villains could be booed and heroes cheered, damsels could have their distress relieved and the good cause emerge triumphant.

All was either black or white, good versus evil, no room for shades of grey, nothing complicated, and no one to explain away the villain's evil ways with tales of a deprived childhood. It was kept simple; put it on horseback and throw in a few wild animals. Fast and furious at Astley's, horses galloping, guns firing, animals escaping, to the thrills and edification of the audience. It was an immediate success, and like the touring waxworks, a fertile source for the potters inspiration.

Dogs

Queen Victoria kept King Charles Spaniels as pets and a particular favourite of hers was a dog called 'Dash' and it is believed that he was the initial inspiration for the thousand upon thousand of Comforter dogs that were made. They were certainly popular, coming in many shapes and sizes, usually in pairs. Today these figures are recognised as typical Staffordshire. Not only were King Charles spaniels potted but a whole range of breeds, from Whippets to Bull Mastiff's, Poodles to St. Bernard's. Combining children with dogs was to ensure a wider market for the figures, as sentimentality improved sales.

By the 1880's many of the figures of dogs produced were in the white, with bright gold gilding applied, and in a number of cases with glass eyes glued in, this is a certain way of dating as glass eyes were never used on the figures prior to 1875.

The Pekinese was a new model as this breed is not found in figures before 1875 and dogs standing on four legs without a base were a post 1875 innovation as was the use of underglaze brown that was applied to a number of the new models.

The Catalogue

Chapter 1: Portraits

From the early 1840's until 1875 over one hundred and ten personalities were potted, many in more than one version. After 1875 there was a decline both in the quality and number of figures made, and the number of new personalities potted were very few. The Wilkinson jugs excepted, the majority of the portrait figures made after 1875 were in the white and the enamel colours and underglaze blue that was used in the previous period were discontinued.

There were exceptions and a few continued to be coloured, most of these emanate from The Parr-Kent Pottery which continued producing a number of portrait figures which had first been made in the 1850's and 1860's. Garibaldi and its pair Napier (**See Victorian Staffordshire Figures 1835-1875, Figs. 139 & 216**) standing by their horses are a case in point. The early figures have a combed green and brown coloured base, by the 1880's whilst the bases are still green and brown, the paint has been applied more heavily and is coated rather than decorated and the combing has disappeared.

Where we have been unable to illustrate a known portrait figure, a full description has been given and it has been allocated a figure number. The pairs have been cross-referenced against each other, giving the name of its pair and its figure number.

Where a figure has been illustrated in our earlier books, 'Victorian Staffordshire Figures 1835-1875' we have given the original figure number.

When the source of a figure has been illustrated, it keeps the same figure number, but has the letters **SO** by it.

For Quick Reference

P = The figure has a pair
S = The figure is part of a series
SO = The source to the figure

List of Persons Portrayed

The British and Foreign Royalty

1. Queen Victoria
2. King Edward VII
   (The Prince of Wales)
3. Queen Alexandra
4. Queen Mary (Princess May of Teck)
5. Albert Duke of Clarence
6. King George V
7. Shah Nasred Din of Persia
8. Alexander II Tsar of Russia
9. Abdul Hamid II Sultan of Turkey
10. King William III
11. Queen Mary (Wife of William III)

Other Personalities

B
12. Baden – Powell Robert
13. Beatty, Sir David
14. Botha, Louis
15. Booth, William
16. Buller Sir Redvers Henry
17. Burnaby, Frederick Gustavus
C
18. Cavell, Edith
19. Churchill, Winston Spencer
20. Cochrane, Douglas (Lord Dundonald)
21. Connaught, Arthur (Duke of)
D
22. DeWet, Christian
23. Disraeli, Benjamin
F
24. Fitzgerald, Lord Edward
25. Foch, Ferdinand
26. French, John Denton Pinkstone
G
27. Gladstone, Catherine
28. Gladstone, William Ewart
29. Gordon, Charles George
H
30. Haig, Sir Douglas
J
31. Jellicoe, Sir John
32. Joffre, Joseph
K
33. Kitchener, Horatio Herbert
L
34. Lloyd, George David
M
35. McCracken, Henry Joy
36. Macdonald, Sir Hector Archibald
N
37. Nelson, Horatio
P
38. Parnell, Charles Stewart
R
39. Roberts, Evan
40. Roberts, Lord Frederick Sleigh
S
41. Sarsfield, Patrick (Earl of Lucan)
42. Sexton, Thomas
43. Stewart, Sir Herbert
T
44. Tone, Theobald Wolfe
W
45. Wilson, Woodrow
46. Wolseley, Garnet Joseph

The British and Foreign Royalty

1. Queen Victoria (1819–1901)

Alexandrina Victoria succeeded to the throne on the death of her uncle William IV in 1837 at the age of eighteen and then reigned for sixty-four years until her death in 1901. In 1840 she married Albert, Prince of Saxe-Coberg-Gotha, her second cousin. She had nine children, four sons and five daughters in sixteen years. Albert died prematurely in 1861 and the Queen remained in mourning for him for the rest of her life. In 1876 she became Empress of India, in 1887 she celebrated her Golden Jubilee and in 1897 her Diamond Jubilee.

Fig. 4000
A figure of Queen Victoria standing, crowned in full-length dress with garter sash, hands clasped together in front.
Two other adapted figures can be found. The first is titled 'QUEEN OF ENGLAND & EMPRESS OF INDIA CROWNED JUNE 20TH 1837 YEAR OF JUBILEE 1897', this figure is 16 inches high. (Figure 4001 has been reserved for it.)
The second is very rare, titled 'QUEEN VICTORIA CROWNED JUNE 20TH 1837 YEARS OF JUBILEE 1887-97 DIED JAN 22ND 1901, This figure is 15.5 inches high. (Figure 4002 has been reserved for it.)
HEIGHT: 16.75. inches
TITLE: QUEEN OF ENGLAND & EMPRESS OF INDIA CROWNED JUNE 20TH 1837 YEAR OF JUBILEE 1887
PRICE: F

2. King Edward VII (The Prince of Wales) (1841-1910)

The eldest son of Queen Victoria and Prince Albert he married Princess Alexandra of Denmark in 1862, he succeeded to the throne at the age of 60 on the death of his mother Queen Victoria in 1901, he reigned for 9 years until his death in 1910 when he was succeeded by his son George V.

3. Queen Alexandra (Wife of King Edward VII) (1844-1925)

Eldest daughter of King Christian IX of Denmark married the then Prince of Wales in 1863 became Queen on his accession to the throne in 1901.

Fig. 552
A figure of Queen Victoria, standing, crowned in full-length dress with garter sash, hands clasped together in front.
This figure was first made in about 1870, and is included in our previous book V.S.F 1835-1875, This figure pairs with the Prince of Wales, it has been included in this subsequent book, as no less than three debased versions were later derived from it. There is no record however of the pair, the Prince of Wales, being made in debased smaller versions to pair these later figures.
HEIGHT: 17.5 inches
TITLE: QUEEN OF ENGLAND
PRICE: E

Fig. 4003P
A figure of King Edward VII, titled in raised capitals, mounted on horseback, dressed in military uniform with a cocked hat, his right hand on his hip, his left holding the reins.
This figure was made by Lancaster and pairs with Queen Alexandra (See figure 4004).
HEIGHT: 13.25 inches.
TITLE: KING EDWARD VII
PRICE: F

Fig. 4004P
A figure of Queen Alexandra, titled in raised capitals, mounted on horseback, wearing a bowler hat, bodice and full length riding dress, both hands holding the reins, which are across her lap.
This figure was made by Lancaster and pairs with King Edward VII (See figure 4003).
HEIGHT: 12.75 inches.
TITLE: QUEEN ALEXANDRA
PRICE: F

Fig. 4005P
A figure of King Edward VII, titled in raised capitals, standing bareheaded in military uniform, a cocked hat held in his right hand, his left resting on a sword a twisted pillar is to his right. This figure is illustrated in colour; it is much more common to find it in the white.
This figure was made by Lancaster and pairs with Queen Alexandra (See figure 4006).
HEIGHT: 13 inches
TITLE: KING EDWARD VII
PRICE: F

Fig. 4006P
A figure of Queen Alexandra, titled in raised capitals, standing crowned, her hands clasped in front holding a fan, wearing a full-length dress with a sash.
This figure was made by Lancaster and pairs with King Edward VII (See figure 4005).
HEIGHT: 13 inches
TITLE: QUEEN ALEXANDRA
PRICE: F

Fig. 4007P
A figure of King Edward VII, titled in indented capitals, standing, wearing a plumed hat and a long cloak over a military uniform, holding a scroll in his left hand, his right on his hip a sword hanging from his belt.
This figure was made by Kent and pairs with Queen Alexandra (See figure 4008).
HEIGHT: 14 inches
TITLE: KING EDWARD VII
PRICE: F

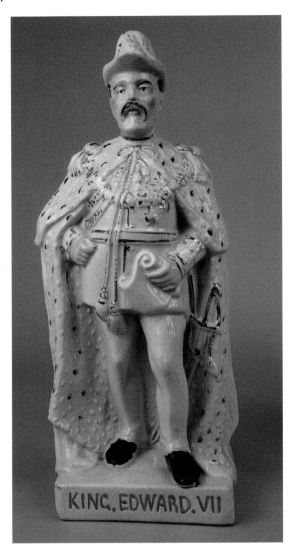

Fig. 4008P
A figure of Queen Alexandra, titled in indented capitals, standing crowned, dressed in a veil and cloak over a full-length dress with a sash
This figure was made by Kent and pairs with King Edward VII (See figure 4007).
HEIGHT: 14 inches
TITLE: QUEEN ALEXANDRA
PRICE: F

Fig. 4008SO
A coloured print of King Edward VII and Queen Alexandra, the depiction of Edward is very similar to Figure 4005 and Alexandra is very similar to Figure 4008, either may be the source or inspiration for these figures.

Fig. 4009P
(Not illustrated) A figure of King Edward VII, titled in gilt script, standing wearing a cocked hat and cloak over a military uniform, and holding a scroll his right hand.
This figure pairs with Queen Alexandra (See figure 4010).
This figure is identical in all respects to Figure 4007, other than the titling, it being almost a mirror image, i.e. he is holding the scroll in his right, not left hand, and the titling is in gilt script not indented capitals.
This is a very rare figure with only three examples having been recorded.
HEIGHT: 14.5 inches
TITLE: KING OF ENGLAND
PRICE: F

Fig. 4010P
(Not illustrated) A figure of Queen Alexandra, titled in gilt script, standing, wearing a crown, a veil, and an ermine edged cloak over a full-length dress, holding a fan in her left hand
This figure pairs with King Edward VII (See figure 4009).
This figure is similar in most respects, other than titling and the positions of her hands to Figure 4008
HEIGHT: 14.5 inches
TITLE: QUEEN OF ENGLAND
PRICE: F

4. Queen Mary (Princess May of Teck) (1867-1953)

The daughter of Francis of Teck and the granddaughter of Adolphus The Duke of Cambridge she was first engaged to Albert, The Duke of Clarence but he died before their marriage, she then married his brother George who was then heir apparent and subsequently became King George V.

5. Albert, Duke of Clarence (1864-1892)

The eldest son of King Edward VII, and, therefore the future King, he was engaged to Princess May of Teck but died before the wedding.

Fig. 4012P
A figure of The Duke of Clarence, titled in raised capitals, standing, dressed in belted jacket and trousers, a sash over his left shoulder, his right hand resting on his hip, his left resting on the barrel of a cannon behind him, cannon balls are stacked on the base.
This figure pairs with Princess May (See figure 4011).
HEIGHT: 15.75 inches
TITLE: DUKE OF CLARENCE
PRICE: F

Fig. 4011P
A figure of Princess May, titled in raised capitals, standing in full-length dress, her left hand resting on a pillar, her right to her waist, a fan suspended from her wrist.
This figure pairs with Duke of Clarence (See figure 4012).
HEIGHT: 15.75 inches
TITLE: PRINCESS MAY
PRICE: F

6. King George V (1865-1936)

The second son of Edward VII, succeeded to the throne in 1910, becoming heir apparent due to the premature death of his brother the Duke of Clarence in 1892, married Princess May of Teck in 1893, who had previously been engaged to his brother. He was King during the First World War of 1914 to 1918.

Fig. 4013S
A figure of George V, seated moustached and bearded dressed in a sailor's uniform holding a globe of the world, a lion seated either side forms the arms to the chair, the whole in the form of a jug.
This figure is part of the series of twelve character jugs made by Wilkinson Ltd. and was limited to an edition of 1000 figures.
HEIGHT: 12 inches
TITLE: PRO PATRIA
PRICE: E

7. Shah Nasred Din of Persia (1829-1896)

Acceded to the throne of Persia in 1848, visiting England in 1873, where he was received and entertained by the Prince of Wales, his was a popular visit and a song was penned in his honour, the title of which 'Have you seen The Shah' became a catchword, Visited England again in 1889. Was responsible for the introduction of European ideas into the Muslim world of Persia, making him extremely unpopular, and as a result he was assassinated in 1896.

Fig. 4015
A figure of Shah Nasred Din, titled in raised capitals, mounted on horseback wearing a fez with a plume and military uniform with a sash over his shoulder, his left hand holding the reins on the horse's neck.
This figure can be found with the Shah's face blackened, and the figure has never been recorded in colour.
This is a right hand side figure, i.e. the horse is facing left and there should therefore be a pair, if it exists it would probably be a mirror image, one has not been recorded however, in the event that one exists, Figure 4014 has been reserved for it.
HEIGHT: 15.25. inches
TITLE: HAVE YOU SEEN THE SHAH
PRICE: E

Figs. 4016/4017

(Not Illustrated) A pair of figures of Shah Nasred Din, titled in raised capitals, mounted on horseback, wearing a fez with a plume and military uniform with a sash over his shoulder, one hand is placed on the horse's flank and the other on the saddlecloth.
These figures can be found either with an unattractive 'orange peel' finish, or on rare occasions they are nicely coloured, and were made by Sampson Smith.
Figure 4016 is similar to Figure 4015, other than being a mirror image, the placement of the hands, design of the saddlecloth and the size.
HEIGHT: 13.5 inches
TITLE: HAVE YOU SEEN THE SHAH
PRICE: Pair E, Singles F

8. Alexander II, Tsar of Russia (1818-1881)

The son of the Emperor Nicholas I, succeeded to the throne in 1855 during the Crimean War, his only daughter Marie married Alfred Duke of Edinburgh the son of Queen Victoria, in 1877 he led his armies in the war against the Turks, dying in 1881 due to injuries caused when a bomb was thrown at him.

Fig. 4019
A figure of Shah Nasred Din mounted on horseback wearing a fez with a plume and military uniform his right hand placed on the horse's neck, the saddlecloth is very long reaching the ground.
This figure has only been recorded facing left it is possible that a pair to it facing right was made, so Figure 4018 has been reserved for it.
This is probably a smaller version of Figure 4017 but it has never been recorded titled.
HEIGHT: 10 inches
PRICE: G

Fig. 4020P
A figure of Alexander II Tsar of Russia, titled in gilt script, seated on horseback facing right, with moustache and sideburns, wearing a plumed hat and military uniform, his left hand holding the horse's reins, his right placed on the horses flank, holding a script.
Both titled and untitled figures can be found.
This figure and its pair were made by Sampson Smith and portray the principal opponents in the Russo- Turkish War of 1877-78.
HEIGHT: 14.5 inches
TITLE: EMPEROR OF RUSSIA
PRICE: E

9. Abdul Hamid II, Sultan of Turkey (1842-1918)

Succeeded to the throne in 1876, a deeply distrustful man he extracted his own teeth, prepared his own medicines and had tasters check his food, oppressing his Christian subjects, causing the war between Turkey and Russia of 1877-1878. Turkey was defeated; his mis-rule causing his exile in 1909.

Fig. 4021P
A figure of Abdul Hamid II, Sultan of Turkey, titled in gilt script, mounted on horseback, wearing a fez with tassel and a military uniform with sword, holding the reins in his right hand and a scroll in his left.

The figure illustrated is not titled, but titled figures were produced, they are more often found titled when the base of the figures have been left uncoloured.

This figure and its pair The Tsar, are amongst the finest of the later figures produced, the modelling and colouring being particularly good.

Two figures are illustrated, both were made by Sampson Smith, identical apart from decoration, both are Circa 1877/8.
HEIGHT: 14.5 inches
TITLE: SULTAN OF TURKEY
PRICE: E

10. King William III (1650-1702)

A Dutchman, in 1677 he married his cousin Mary, the daughter of James II of England, The English, dissatisfied with the Catholic King James, invited the Protestant William Prince of Orange and together with his wife they landed in Devon in 1688. Parliament declared the throne vacant and in 1689 William and Mary were declared King and Queen. James went to France and in 1689 with the help of French mercenaries invaded Ireland in an attempt to regain his throne. Defeated at the Battle of the Boyne in 1690 and fled back to France, William and Mary had no children and on William's death, Mary's sister Anne subsequently became Queen.

11. Queen Mary II (1662-1694)

The daughter of James II married William the Prince of Orange in 1677. Unlike her father she was a Protestant; forced by circumstances to choose between her father and her husband, she chose her husband and became Queen in 1689, dying of smallpox in 1694.

Figs 727/728
A pair of figures of Queen Mary II and King William III on horseback, on titled bases with raised gilt capitals, Queen Mary with her left arm across her chest, her right holding the reins, wearing a bonnet with scarf, bodice and long skirt. King William with his right arm resting on the horse's mane, holding a scroll, his left to his side above a sword, wearing a plumed hat, ermine sleeved jacket, breeches and knee boots.
Most of the William III and Mary figures can be found decorated with either bright or best gold and can therefore be dated to a period either side of 1875.
These figures were also included in V.S.F. Book One, as they straddled the period; the pair in Book One are in full colour, we have kept the same numbers for the white pair illustrated, which were probably made in the late 1870's.
HEIGHT: 10.5 inches
TITLE: QUEEN MARY - KING WILLIAM III
PRICE: Pair E, Singles F

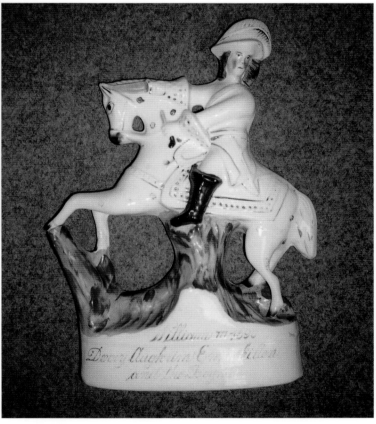

Figs. 4022/4023P
A pair of figures of King William III, titled in gilt script, seated on a horse that is rearing, wearing a plumed hat long coat and knee boots, holding in his left hand a short sword pointing forward, and in his right a pistol.
A matched pair are illustrated one has a coloured base one has not.
HEIGHT: 14.75 inches
TITLE: WILLIAM 111 1690, DERRY AUGHRIM ENNISKILLEN AND THE BOYNE
PRICE: Pair E, Singles F

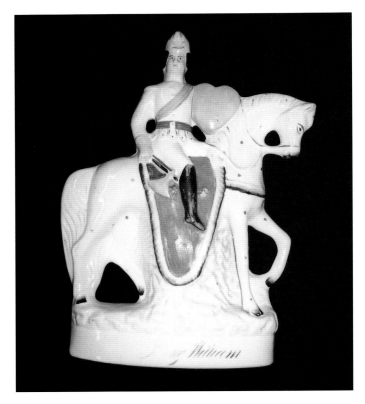

Fig 4024
A figure of King William III, titled in gilt script, mounted on horse back, with a long saddlecloth, wearing a helmet, tunic with sash and belt and trousers with knee boots, holding a heart shaped shield in his left hand, and a battleaxe in his right.
This figure is one of a pair, an almost mirror image figure can be found, it is not usually titled and this is the only figure that the authors have seen titled 'King William' and it is probable that the potter realising that there was a market for King William III figures took a stock figure and applied a title, it is unlikely that King William would have used a battleaxe.
There is a pair to this figure, 4025 has been reserved for it.
HEIGHT: 13 inches
TITLE: KING WILLIAM
PRICE: F

Fig. 4027P
A figure King William III, titled in gilt script, seated on horseback, wearing a plumed hat, long coat and knee boots, his right hand on the horse's neck, holding a scroll, his left holding the reins.
This figure can be found in two sizes, 9.75 inch version illustrated.
This figure pairs with Queen Mary II (See figure 4026). Both this figure and its pair usually have the script and gilding in bright gold, the pair illustrated are however decorated with best gold and this would date them to pre 1875.
HEIGHT: 9.25 inches, 9.75 inches.
TITLE: KING WILLIAM 3RD
PRICE: F

Fig. 4026P
A figure of Queen Mary II, titled in gilt script, seated on horseback, wearing a plumed hat, ermine edged coat and long dress, both hands resting in her lap.
The precise date of this figure and its pair is uncertain; mostly the figures are found titled in bright gold but on occasion figures have been found titled in best gold.
This figure can be found in two sizes, 9.5 inch version illustrated.
This figure pairs with King William III (See figure 4027)
HEIGHT: 9 inches, 9.5 inches
TITLE: MARY 2
PRICE: F

Fig. 4029
A figure of King William III, titled in gilt script, mounted on horseback, wearing a plumed hat, jacket, and knee boots, holding a scroll in his right hand on the horse's neck, a sword hanging at his waist. The horse is rearing with its front hooves on rockwork.
This figure can be found in two sizes, an 11 inch version is illustrated, and its pair would be either a mirror image or a figure of Queen Mary II (although it has not been recorded in either size, though it probably exists). (Figure 4028 has been reserved for it).
A variation of this figure can be found which has modelling differences the main being that only one of the front legs of the horse is raised, its tail is longer and continues under the back leg, no pair has been recorded for this figure either.
HEIGHT: 11 inches, 12 inches
TITLE: KING WILLIAM 3ᴿᴰ
PRICE: F

Other Personalities

12. Baden-Powell, Robert Stephenson Smyth (1857-1941)

After serving in India with the 13th Hussars he was sent to South Africa in 1899 to raise regiments to fight against the Boers. Held Mafeking during its siege until its relief in May 1900, in which year he was promoted to Major General. He is best known for founding the Boy Scout and Girl Guide movement.

Fig. 4030
A figure of King William III, titled in gilt script, mounted on horseback, wearing a plumed hat, jacket with decorations and cross belted, long trousers with shoes, holding the reins in his left hand, his right is on the horse's neck holding a scroll.
Once again no pair has been recorded for this figure, although one may exist, this figure is similar to Figure 4027, the main difference being that he is wearing long trousers and shoes not knee boots.
HEIGHT: 11 inches
TITLE: KING WILLIAM 3ᴿᴰ
PRICE: F

Fig. 4031P
A figure of Baden Powell, titled in gilt capitals, mounted on horseback, his left hand holding the horses reins, his right on the flank of the horse, wearing a wide brimmed hat military uniform with knee boots.
This figure is part of a series of eight made by the Kent-Parr factory, the first pair Wolseley, (See figure 4111) and Gordon, (See figure 4077) in 1898 to commemorate Wolseley's attempt to relieve Gordon at Khartoum. The second pair Kitchener, (See figure 4086) and McDonald, (See figure 4093) to commemorate the Battle of Omdurman in 1898. The final two pairs were made in 1898/1900 to commemorate battles in the Boer War, they were figures of French, (See figure 4064), Roberts, (See figure 4101), Baden-Powell, (See figure 4031) and Buller, (See figure 4039).
This figure pairs with Buller (See figure 4039).
HEIGHT: 14.5 inches
TITLE: BADEN POWELL
PRICE: F

Fig. 4033P
A figure of Baden Powell, titled by raised capitals on a plaque, mounted on horseback, in brimmed hat and military uniform, his left hand across his chest holding the horses reins, his right on the horses flank.
This figure pairs with Macdonald (See figure 4095).
There are a further five figures in this series, they can all be identified by the method of applying the title via a plaque with 'v' ends. The figures are French, (See figure 4063), Kitchener, (See figure 4088), McDonald, (See figure 4095), Roberts, (See figure 4103) and Buller (See figure 4041).
These figures can be found made by either the press or slip mould methods, press mould figures have been found with a factory mark 'SADLER/BURSLEM/ENGLAND
HEIGHT: 12 inches
TITLE: BADEN-POWELL
PRICE: F

Fig. 4032
A figure of Baden Powell, titled in gilt script standing in a brimmed hat, belted jacket and trousers a bandolier over his shoulder, a sword on his belt, his right hand on his hip his left hand resting on a cannon, there are cannon balls stacked on the base.
This figure is a modification of the figure of the Duke of Clarence (See figure 4012).
HEIGHT: 16.5 inches
TITLE: BADEN POWELL
PRICE: F

13. Beatty, Admiral Sir David (1871-1936)

Born in Nantwich Cheshire and joined the Royal Navy in 1884, served in the Sudan and the China War of 1900 where he developed a reputation for aggressive warfare. By 1912 he was in command of the 1ˢᵗ Battle cruiser Squadron. During the First World War his tactics achieved success at Heligoland Blight in 1914 and at Dogger Bank in 1915. When Jellicoe was criticised for his defensive tactics towards sea warfare, Beatty was appointed his replacement. This caused resentment as this promotion was over the heads of eight more senior admirals. In the event he was unwilling to seek a major confrontation with the German Navy, believing that his main concern should be the preservation of the Dreadnoughts. Appointed First Sea Lord in 1919 and held this post until his retirement in 1927, when he was created a peer.

Fig. 4034S
A titled figure of Beatty seated dressed in full naval uniform holding a large shell between his legs.
This figure in the form of a jug is part of the series of twelve made by Wilkinson Ltd. and was limited to an edition of 350 figures.
HEIGHT: 11 inches
TITLE: DREADNOUGHT
PRICE: E

14. Botha, Louis (1862-1919)

Born in Greytown, Natal, elected to the Transvaal Volksraad in 1897, he was South Africa's most impressive military leader during the Boer War of 1899-1902. His success at Spion Kop resulted in his being promoted to commander-in-chief of the Boer forces. After signing the Vereeniging Peace Treaty in 1902 he worked tirelessly for reconciliation with Britain. In 1907 he was elected Prime Minister of the Transvaal Colony under the new constitution and three years later became the first president of South Africa. On the outbreak of the First World War, he offered to send troops to invade German South-West Africa. Afrikaner opposition to this provoked a major Boer revolt. This was defeated, but it weakened Botha's position and in the elections of 1915 his party only narrowly held on to power. From July 1915 Botha passed direct military power to Jan Smuts. At the end of the First World War he attended the Paris Peace Conference and argued against the harsh treatment of Germany, he was however a signatory of the Versailles Treaty, he died shortly after in 1919.

Fig. 4035S
A figure of Botha seated, dressed in military uniform holding a jug on his left knee.
This figure in the form of a jug is part of the series of twelve made by Wilkinson Ltd in a limited edition.
HEIGHT: 11 inches
TITLE: LOYALTY
PRICE: E

15. Booth, William (1829-1912)

Started working life as an assistant to a pawnbroker in Nottingham, in his early twenties he became an itinerant preacher, subsequently coming to London and opening a Mission in Whitechapel where 'down and outs' were looked after. He created the Salvation Army, a temperance organisation, which survives to this day. It gave its members military titles, and dressed them in pseudo military uniform; as its head he took the title 'General Booth.'

Fig. 4036/4037
Left: A bust of Booth, wearing a Salvation army cap and uniform and has a long beard, on his cap band is inscribed 'The Salvation Army. **This figure could not have been made earlier than the 1890's and is unusual in that it is invariably in underglaze blue. Booth's granddaughter was of the opinion that this figure was made in 1912 to commemorate his death. It is a hollow base figure made by the slip mould method.**
This is an extremely rare figure and consequently can be very expensive, the last time this figure appeared at auction in January 2002 it made over £4200, ($5900). Another example was sold by a dealer some five years previously for £1500 ($2100).
HEIGHT: 14 inches
PRICE: A/B

Bottom: A bust of Booth on a pedestal base, wearing the uniform of the Salvation Army but is bareheaded, the letters 'SALV' appear indented on his shirtfront.
This figure, which is extremely rare, is also likely to have been produced to commemorate his death.
The figure is illustrated together with a larger version, Figure 4036.
HEIGHT: 9.75 inches
PRICE: D

16. Buller, Sir Redvers Henry (1839-1908)

Eton educated, gaining a commission into the army in 1858, served in The Red River expedition in 1870, commanded The Frontier Light Horse in the sixth Kaffir War of 1878/9, receiving the highest award, The Victoria Cross for gallantry. He was Chief of Staff to Wolseley in the campaign to relieve Gordon at Khartoum, and was awarded a knighthood in 1885, made a general in 1896, he was commander in chief of the Boer War until his defeat at Colenso in 1899 when he was replaced by Lord Roberts.

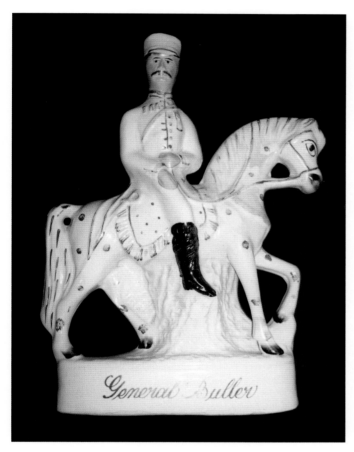

Fig. 4038P
A figure of General Buller, titled in gilt script, mounted on horseback, in military uniform with a peaked a cap.
This figure pairs with Macdonald (See figure 4092).
This figure is part of a series of ten figures made by Sampson Smith all of which are very rare. The series consists of a pair of figures titled '21ˢᵗ Lancers, Buller, (See figure 4038), Kitchener (See figures 4084, 4085), McDonald, See figures 4091, 4092), Dundonald, (See figure 4048), Roberts, (See figure 4100), and French (See figure 4061).
HEIGHT: 11 inches
TITLE: GENERAL BULLER
PRICE: F

Fig. 4039P
A titled figure of General Buller, titled in capitals mounted on horseback, wearing a military uniform with peaked cap and knee boots, his right hand on his hip holding the reins, his left on his thigh.
This figure pairs with Baden-Powell, (See figure 4031).
This figure is part of a series of eight made by the Kent-Parr factory, the first pair Wolseley, (See figure 4111) and Gordon, (See figure 4077) in 1898 to commemorate Wolseley's attempt to relieve Gordon at Khartoum. The second pair Kitchener, (See figure 4086) and McDonald (See figure 4093) to commemorate the Battle of Omdurman in 1898. The final two pairs were made in 1898/1900 to commemorate battles in the Boer War, they were figures of French (See figure 4064), Roberts, (See figure 4101), Baden-Powell, (See figure 4031) and Buller, (See figure 4039).
HEIGHT: 14.75 inches
TITLE: BULLER
PRICE: F

Fig. 4040P
A figure of General Buller, titled in gilt script, mounted on horseback, in military uniform of peaked cap jacket, breeches and knee boots, his right hand holding a scroll on the horse's mane, his left holding the reins.
This figure pairs with General Roberts (See figure 4102). There are a further five figures in this series which were all made by Sampson Smith to commemorate the commanders in the Boer War, they are usually found in the white but can be found coloured as illustrated.
The complete series consists of Buller, (See figure 4040), Roberts, (See figure 4102), Dundonald (See figure 4049), McDonald, (See figure 4094), Kitchener, (See figure 4087) and French, (See figure 4062).
HEIGHT: 14 inches
TITLE: GENERAL BULLER
PRICE: F

17. Burnaby, Frederick Gustavus (1842-1885)

A cavalry officer, he had many talents, amongst them being a linguist who spoke five languages, he was also a balloonist and author, joined Wolseley's expedition in 1884 and was killed in action in the attempt to relieve Khartoum.

Fig. 4041P
A figure of General Buller, titled in raised capitals on a plaque, mounted on horseback, in military uniform of peaked cap jacket and breeches, his right hand on the horses flank, his left holding the reins.
This figure pairs with General Roberts, (See figure 4103). There are a further five figures in this series, they can all be identified by the method of applying the title via a plaque with 'v' ends. The figures are French, (See figure 4063), Kitchener, (See figure 4088), McDonald, (See figure 4095), Roberts, (See figure 4103) and Baden-Powell, (See figure 4033).
These figures can be found made by either the press or slip mould methods, press mould figures have been found with a factory mark 'SADLER/BURSLEM/ENGLAND.
HEIGHT: 12 inches
TITLE: SIR REDVERS BULLER
PRICE: F

Fig. 4043P
A figure of Burnaby, titled in raised capitals, mounted on horseback, dressed in full military uniform of high helmet, jacket and knee boots, his right hand on the horse's mane, his left on his thigh.
This figure pairs with Stewart, (See figure 4106).
This figure and its pair were memorial figures as both Burnaby and Stewart died of their wounds incurred in the campaign to relieve Gordon at Khartoum.
Two figures are illustrated, one in part colour one in the white, the blue used to colour his tunic is overglaze enamel, this is the only figure to have been made of Burnaby.
HEIGHT: 15.5 inches
TITLE: C BURNABY
PRICE: F

18. Cavell, Edith (1866-1915)

A British nurse, the Matron at the Berkendael Medical Institute, during the First World War it became a Red Cross Hospital, and she attended both German and allied wounded. In 1915 she was arrested by the Germans and charged with assisting allied soldiers to escape. She confessed that she had been successful in so doing and was condemned to death by German Court Martial; she was shot by firing squad in October 1915.

Fig. 4045
A figure of a woman standing dressed in nurses uniform with bow tie, her hands clasped in front, a pair of scissors hanging from her left wrist and a bag from her right, a cross is on the front of her uniform.
This figure is made from a slip mould as opposed to a press mould, and apart from the Wilkinson jugs is the only figure made of First World War personalities, it is also possible that this is not a portrait of Cavell, the identification is solely based on the uniform which is of The London Hospital where Cavell trained in 1895.
It has never been recorded other than in the white and has a hollow base, is of little quality but is extremely rare.
HEIGHT: 9.75 inches
PRICE: F

19. Churchill, Winston Spencer (1874 -1965)

The son of Lord Randolph Churchill and the American Jennie Jerome, born at Blenheim Palace, educated at Harrow and Sandhurst he became an officer in the Fourth Hussars. Saw action on the Indian North- West frontier where he took part in the Battle of Omdurman. He left the army and became a war correspondent. Whilst reporting the Boer War he was taken prisoner, making headline news when he escaped, returning to England he wrote a book about his experiences ('London to Ladysmith'). Stood for Parliament in 1900 and was elected a Conservative M. P. for Oldham, switching to the Liberal Party and in the 1906 election took the seat for North-West Manchester and entered government as Under-Secretary of State for the Colonies. In 1910 he became Home Secretary and in 1911 was appointed First Lord of the Admiralty. Churchill was one of the first to recognise the potential of aeroplanes in war and in 1912 set up the Royal Naval Air Service.

On the outbreak of war in 1914 he joined the War Council; he was however blamed for the failure at Dardanelles and was moved to the post of Chancellor of the Dutchy of Lancaster. Unhappy, he rejoined the army and commanded a battalion of The Royal Scots Fusiliers on the Western Front. He was brought back into government and for the final year of the war was Minister of Munitions.

After the war he served in the government of Lloyd George, by 1924 he had left the Liberal party and re-joined the Conservatives remaining in parliament, but by 1930 was not in the government, spending the next few years writing.

With the outbreak of the Second World war he was appointed First Lord of the Admiralty, and when Chamberlain resigned in May 1940 Churchill replaced him as Prime Minister, forming a coalition government to unite behind the war effort. On the election after the war he was surprisingly defeated by the Labour party led by Clement Attlee.

He returned to power in the election of 1951, but was not a well man and retired from office in 1955. He was awarded the Nobel Prize for Literature for his six-volume work '*The Second World War.*'

Fig. 4047S
A titled figure of Churchill seated in full uniform holding a ship in his arms a bulldog seated below him. This figure is in the form of a jug and is part of a series of twelve made by Wilkinson Ltd.
**This figure was made much later than the other eleven and was an afterthought to make up an even dozen figures. Whilst the eleven were made circa 1914/1918 it was not until 1941 that this figure was made. It is now even more desirable than the other eleven as it was designed and signed by Clarice Cliffe, in a limited edition, so it is now in demand by collectors of Staffordshire, Military, Churchillian, and Clarice Cliffe.
This figure can be found sparsely coloured or in full colour, both variations are illustrated.**
HEIGHT: 11.5 inches
TITLE: MAY.GOD.DEFEND.THE.RIGHT
PRICE: D

20. Cochrane, Douglas Mackinnon Baillie Hamilton (Lord Dundonald) (1852-1935)

Began his military career in the Lifeguards, his rides with despatches recording the fall of Khartoum and the death of Gordon made him famous, became the 12th Lord Dundonald in 1885, fought in the Boer War and commanded the 2nd Cavalry Brigade in the relief of Ladysmith, becoming a General in 1906.

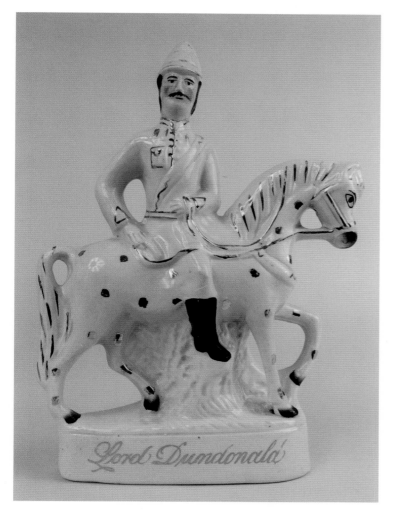

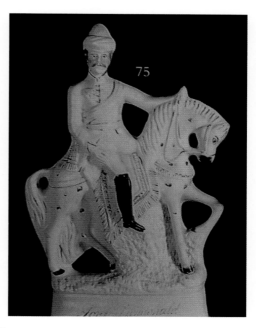

Fig. 4048P
A figure of Lord Dundonald titled in gilt script, mounted on horseback, dressed in full military uniform of helmet, jacket with belt, breeches and knee boots, his right hand on the horses flank.
This figure pairs with French (See figure 4061).
This figure is part of a series of ten figures made by Sampson Smith all of which are very rare. The series consists of a pair of figures titled '21ˢᵗ Lancers, Buller, (See figure 4038), Kitchener, (See figures 4084, 4085), McDonald, (See figures 4091, 4092), Dundonald, (See figure 4048), Roberts, (See figure 4100), and French, (See figure 4061).
This figure is identical to Roberts (Figure 4100) other than titling.
HEIGHT: 10.5 inches
TITLE: LORD DUNDONALD
PRICE: F

Fig. 4049P
A figure of Lord Dundonald titled in gilt script mounted on horseback facing right dressed in full military uniform of helmet, jacket with a scarf over his shoulder and across his chest, breeches and knee boots, his left hand on the horses mane, his right on his thigh.
This figure pairs with Macdonald (See figure 4094).
This figure is derived from a figure of Wolseley, (See figure 4109), slight changes have been made to the head and the title has been changed.
There are a further five figures in this series which were all made by Sampson Smith to commemorate the commanders in the Boer War, they are usually found in the white but can be found coloured. The complete series consists of Buller, (See figure 4040), Roberts, (See figure 4102), Dundonald, (See figure 4049), McDonald, (See figure 4094), Kitchener, (See figure 4087) and French, (See figure 4062).
HEIGHT: 14.75 inches
TITLE: LORD DUNDONALD
PRICE: F

21. Connaught, Arthur William Patrick (Duke of) (1850-1942)

The third son of Queen Victoria, and became an officer in the Royal Engineers in 1868, his mother created him Duke of Connaught in 1874, and in 1879 he married the daughter of Frederick Charles of Prussia, in 1882 as a Major-general he commanded the 1st Guards brigade under Sir Garnet Wolseley, becoming a Field-marshal in 1902 and The Governor General of Canada in 1911.

Fig. 4050P
A figure of the Duke of Connaught titled in raised capitals, mounted on horseback, dressed in full military uniform of helmet, belted jacket, breeches and knee boots, his right hand on the horses mane, his left on his thigh,
This figure pairs with Wolseley, (See figure 4109).
HEIGHT: 14 inches
TITLE: DUKE OF CONNAUGHT
PRICE: F

Fig. 4051P
A figure of the Duke of Connaught titled in raised capitals mounted on horseback, dressed in full military uniform of helmet, belted jacket, breeches and knee boots, his right hand on the horse's flank, his left across his chest.
This figure and its pair Wolseley, (See figure 4110) are very rare figures.
HEIGHT: 12.5 inches
TITLE: DK. CONNAUGHT
PRICE: E

22. DeWet, Christian (1854-1922)

A Boer General who distinguished himself in the Transvaal War of 1881, he was arguably the most able and certainly the most audacious of the Boer commanders.

Fig. 4053
A figure of DeWet , titled in gilt scrip, standing in front of a large cannon, balls piled by his feet, wearing a slouch hat, jacket with bandolier and trousers, his left hand resting on the barrel of a cannon, his right on his hip.
This figure is identical in all respects other than titling to the figure of Baden-Powell, (See figure 4032), which is in itself an adaptation of the figure of the Duke of Clarence, (See figure 4012) and is an example of the potter using the same mould not twice but three times, the illustration depicts both Baden-Powel and DeWet.
HEIGHT: 16.5 inches
TITLE: DE WET
PRICE: E

23. Disraeli, Benjamin (Earl of Beaconsfield) (1804-1881)

Became a Conservative Member of Parliament in 1837 following a career as an author, he became Britain's only Jewish Prime Minister first in 1868 and then again from 1874-1880, he was a great favourite and friend of Queen Victoria who called him 'Dizzy' and she made him Earl of Beaconsfield in 1876

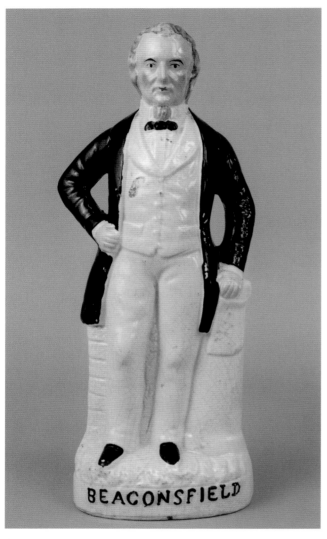

Fig. 4055P
A figure of Disraeli, titled in raised black capitals, standing, dressed in an open frock coat, waistcoat and trousers, his right hand on his hip, his left resting on a pedestal.
This figure pairs with Gladstone (See figure 4069).
HEIGHT: 12 inches
TITLE: BEACONSFIELD
PRICE: E

Fig. 4056P
A figure of Disraeli, titled in gilt script, standing, dressed in frock coat waistcoat and trousers, his left hand resting on a pedestal to his side, his right hand resting on his hip.
This figure pairs with Gladstone Figure 4070.
This figure can be found in two sizes, both illustrated. As both this and the preceding figure are titled 'BEACONSFIELD' they cannot have been made before 1876, as this was the year he was granted the title.
HEIGHT: 14.5, 16.5 inches
TITLE: BEACONSFIELD
PRICE: E

24. Fitzgerald, Lord Edward (1763-1798)

The younger son of the Duke of Leinster, fought for Britain against America in the War of Independence, later he renounced his title and joined United Irishmen, a party whose aims were to secure independence for Ireland from Britain, in this cause he went to France to help arrange a French invasion of Ireland, betrayed and on his return he was captured by the police, during which he received wounds from which he died.

Fig. 4058S
A figure of Lord Fitzgerald, titled in gilt script, standing, dressed in jacket, waistcoat and trousers, his right hand on his hip his left resting on a pillar, on which is inscribed in transfer printed capitals WHO FEARS TO SPEAK OF 98, 1798/1898.
This figure along with Wolfe Tone, (See figure 4106) and McCracken, (See figure 4090) were produced in 1898, 100 years after the event to commemorative the deaths of these three Irish patriots in the abortive uprising of 1798.
This figure is in a series of three with Wolfe Tone, (See figure 4107) and McCracken (See figure 4090).
HEIGHT: 14 inches
TITLE: LORD EDWARD FITZGERALD
PRICE: E

25. Foch, Ferdinand (1851-1929)

Born in Tarbes and fought in the Franco-Prussian War of 1870–1871 was appointed to the French General Staff where he was an artillery specialist. Between 1907 and 1911 he was commandant of the Ecole de Guerre.

Fig. 4059S
A figure of Foch seated dressed in French military uniform, holding a bottle in his left hand and a glass in his right.
This figure is in the form of a jug and is part of a series of twelve figures made by Wilkinson Ltd and was limited to an edition of 500.
HEIGHT: 10 inches
TITLE: AU DIABLE LE KAISER
PRICE: E

26. French, John Denton Pinkstone (Earl of Ypres) (1852-1925)

Joined the navy at the age of 14 in 1866, becoming an army officer in 1874. Served under Wolseley in the relief of Gordon at Khartoum, when the Boer War started he was sent to Natal, where he achieved remarkable success as a cavalry officer, he was made a General in 1902 and a Field Marshall in 1913, he was in supreme command of the British forces in France during the First World War. After the war he was commander of the British home forces and was responsible for dealing with the Easter Rising in 1916. Rewarded with the post of Lord Lieutenant of Ireland he was granted £50000 when he retired in 1921 and was created an Earl.

Fig. 4061P
A figure of French titled in gilt script mounted on horseback facing left, dressed in full military uniform of jacket with belt breeches and knee boots and helmet, his left hand holding the reins his right on the horses saddlecloth.
This figure pairs with Lord Dundonald, (See figure 4048).
This figure is part of a series of ten figures made by Sampson Smith all of which are very rare. The series consists of a pair of figures titled '21ˢᵗ Lancers, Buller, (See figure 4038), Kitchener, (See figure 4084), McDonald, (See figures 4091, 4092), Dundonald, (See figure 4048), Roberts, (See figure 4100) and French, (See figure 4061).
This figure is identical to McDonald (See figure 4092) other than titling.
HEIGHT: 11 inches
TITLE: GENERAL FRENCH
PRICE: F

Fig. 4060S
A figure of French seated dressed in full military uniform holding a jug on his lap, the Union Jack is portrayed on the side of the figure.
This figure is in the form of a jug and is part of a series of twelve figures made by Wilkinson Ltd and was limited to an edition of 350.
HEIGHT: 10 inches
TITLE: FRENCH POUR LES FRANCAIS
PRICE: E

Fig. 4062P
A figure of French titled in gilt script mounted on horseback, dressed in full military uniform of helmet, jacket with epaulettes and belt, breeches and knee boots, his left hand raised to the horses neck holding the reins, his right on his thigh.
Two figures are illustrated one in the white and a much rarer version with a coloured horse and saddlecloth.
This figure pairs with Kitchener, (See figure 4087).
There are a further five figures in this series which were all made by Sampson Smith to commemorate the commanders in the Boer war, they are usually found in the white but can be found coloured as illustrated. The complete series consists of Buller, (See figure 4040), Roberts, (See figure 4102), Dundonald, (See figure 4049), McDonald, (See figure 4094), Kitchener, (See figure 4087) and French, (See figure 4062).
HEIGHT: 14 inches
TITLE: GENERAL FRENCH. (On occasion this figure can be found titled G. FRENCH)
PRICE: F

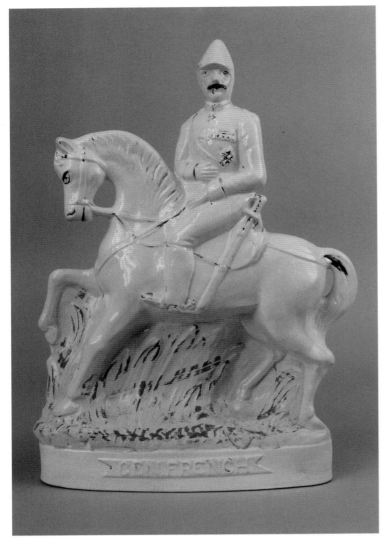

Fig. 4063P
A figure of French titled in raised capitals on a plaque, mounted on horseback, dressed in full military uniform of helmet belted jacket breeches and boots a sword hangs from his waist.
This figure pairs with Kitchener, (See figure 4088).
There are a further five figures in this series, they can all be identified by the method of applying the title via a plaque with 'v' ends. The figures are Buller, (See figure 4041), Kitchener, (See figure 4088), McDonald, (See figure 4095), Roberts, (See figure 4103) and Baden-Powell, (See figure 4033).
These figures can be found made by either the press or slip mould methods, press mould figures have been found with a factory mark 'SADLER/BURSLEM/ENGLAND.'
HEIGHT: 12 inches
TITLE: GEN FRENCH
PRICE: F

Fig. 4064P
A figure of French titled in black capitals, mounted on horseback dressed in military uniform, his left hand is on the horses neck and his right on its flank.
This figure pairs with Roberts, (See figure 4101).
This figure is part of a series of eight made by the Kent-Parr factory, the first pair Wolseley, (See figure 4111) and Gordon, (See figure 4077) in 1898 to commemorate Wolseley's attempt to relieve Gordon at Khartoum. The second pair Kitchener, (See figure 4086) and McDonald, (See figure 4093) to commemorate the Battle of Omdurman in 1898. The final two pairs were made in 1898/1900 to commemorate battles in the Boer War, they were figures of French, (See figure 4064), Roberts, (See figure 4101), Baden-Powell, (See figure 4031) and Buller, (See figure 4039).
HEIGHT: 15 inches
TITLE: FRENCH
PRICE: F

27. Gladstone, Catherine (1813-1900)

Wife of William Ewart Gladstone she married in 1839 and was the daughter of Sir Stephen Glynne.

Fig. 4066P
A figure of Gladstone standing titled in raised capitals, dressed in frockcoat, waistcoat and trousers, his left hand resting on a pillar, his right is to his waist holding a scroll, this is a slip moulded figure.
This figure is illustrated with its pair Catherine Gladstone, (See figure 4065)
HEIGHT: 10.75 inches
TITLE:MR. GLADSTONE
PRICE: F
ROLL NO. 802

Fig. 4067
A figure of Gladstone standing dressed in frockcoat, waistcoat and trousers his left hand holding the lapel of his coat and his right is placed on books, which rests on a pedestal.
Two figures are illustrated, identical apart from decoration, this is one of the better figures produced during this period, the marbling to the base and pillar being particularly attractive.
HEIGHT: 12 inches
PRICE: E

Fig. 4065P
A figure of Catherine Gladstone standing titled in raised capitals, wearing a long dress, a cap on her head and holding a fan, this is a slip-moulded figure.
This figure is illustrated with its pair William Gladstone, (See figure 4066).
HEIGHT: 10.5 inches
TITLE: MRS GLADSTONE
PRICE: F
ROLL NO. 802

28. Gladstone, William Ewart (1809-1908)

A Liberal he entered Parliament in 1832 and held office under Sir Robert Peel, he became Chancellor of the Exchequer in 1852 and was Prime Minister from 1868 to 1874, 1880 to 1886 and finally 1892 to 1894 he was known as the 'Grand Old Man.'

Fig. 4068
(Not Illustrated) A figure of Gladstone standing, dressed in a buttoned three-quarter length overcoat his left hand held to his waist his right by his side.
This is a very rare figure has not been recorded titled and has only been seen in the white.
HEIGHT: 12 inches
PRICE: E

Fig. 4070P
A standing figure of Gladstone, titled in gilt script, dressed in a buttoned frock coat and trousers, his left hand is on his hip and his right holds a sheet of paper and resting on a pedestal, his frock coat is usually coloured in underglaze black.
This figure pairs with Disraeli (See figure 4056).
This figure can be found in two sizes, either titled or untitled, the 14.5 inch version is illustrated.
HEIGHT: 14.5, 16.5 inches
TITLE: GLADSTONE
PRICE: E

Fig. 4069P
A figure of Gladstone titled in raised capitals, standing, dressed in an open frock coat, waistcoat and trousers, his left hand is on his hip and his right hand holds a sheet of paper that is resting upon a pedestal.
This figure usually has the frock coat coloured in underglaze black.
This figure pairs with Disraeli, (See figure 4055).
HEIGHT: 12 inches
TITLE: GLADSTONE
PRICE: E

Fig. 4071
A figure of Gladstone, titled in gilt script, standing, dressed in unbuttoned frock coat, waistcoat and trousers, his right hand holding his lapel, his left holding a sheet of paper and resting on a tree trunk.
HEIGHT: 15.25 inches
TITLE: GLADSTONE
PRICE: E

Fig. 4072P
A figure of Gladstone tiled in raised capitals, standing, dressed in bow tie, frock coat, waistcoat and trousers, his left hand is held to his waist and in his right hand he holds an axe with a tree stump behind, above his left shoulder is a large flag, which is usually decorated as a Union Jack.
This figure pairs with Parnell, (See figure 4097).
This figure and its pair were made to commemorate the Kilmainham Peace Treaty of 1882, between England and Ireland, a centrepiece for this pair was also made of an Angel standing above and behind two women, representing Britannia and Ireland, (See figure 4120) which figure was remodelled in 1902 to commemorate the ending of the Boer War.
HEIGHT: 12.5 inches
TITLE: W. E. GLADSTONE
PRICE: E

29. Gordon, Charles George (1833-1885)

Born in Woolwich, London, enrolling in The Woolwich Academy in 1847, fought in the Crimean War and was wounded at Sebastopol, he also took part in the attack on The Redan, in 1860. He was sent to China and assisted in the capture of Peking, by 1863 he was in charge of the forces in China and took part in over thirty actions against the Taipings, from henceforward he was known as 'Chinese Gordon.' In 1873 he was appointed Governor General in Egypt. In 1884 he was sent to deal with a rebellion organised by The Mahdi, a religious leader who considered that the people had departed from the true path and ways laid down by the Prophet. The Mahdi laid siege to Khartoum and it was defended for nearly a year; finally in January 1885 the Mahdi's men killed Gordon in the palace. Gordon, as well as being an able soldier, was a committed Christian.

Fig. 4075
A figure of Gordon, titled in black capitals, standing dressed in fez, and military uniform, his right hand holding a cane and his left resting on the barrel of a large cannon, which is behind him.
This figure is usually found untitled.
HEIGHT: 16 inches
TITLE: GORDON
PRICE: E

Fig. 4074
A figure of General Gordon titled in indented capitals, seated on a camel, wearing a fez and dressed in jacket and stockings.
The source of this figure is based on the statue by Onslow Ford, which was exhibited at the Royal Academy in 1890. It now stands outside the School of Military Engineering in Chatham in Kent.
HEIGHT: 13.25 inches
TITLE: GENERAL GORDON
PRICE: D

Fig. 4076
A figure of Gordon, titled in raised capitals, standing dressed in fez, military jacket with belt and sash and trousers, his left hand resting on his hip and his right on a tree trunk which is to his side.
Three figures illustrated identical apart from colouring.
HEIGHT: 17.75 inches
TITLE: G. GORDON
PRICE: E

Fig. 4077P
A figure of Gordon, titled in gilt capitals, mounted on horseback, dressed in fez, military jacket, trousers and knee boots, holding the reins, a cane in his right hand, his left is on his thigh.
This figure pairs with Wolseley, (See figure 4111).
This figure is part of a series of eight made by the Kent-Parr Factory, the first pair Wolseley, (See figure 4111) and Gordon, (See figure 4077) in 1898 to commemorate Wolseley's attempt to relieve Gordon at Khartoum. The second pair Kitchener, (See figure 4086) and McDonald, (See figure 4093) to commemorate the Battle of Omdurman in 1898. The final two pairs were made in 1898/1900 to commemorate battles in the Boer War; they were figures of French, (See figure 4064), Roberts, (See figure 4101), Baden-Powell, (See figure 4031) and Buller, (See figure 4039).
HEIGHT: 14.5 inches
TITLE: GORDON
PRICE: F

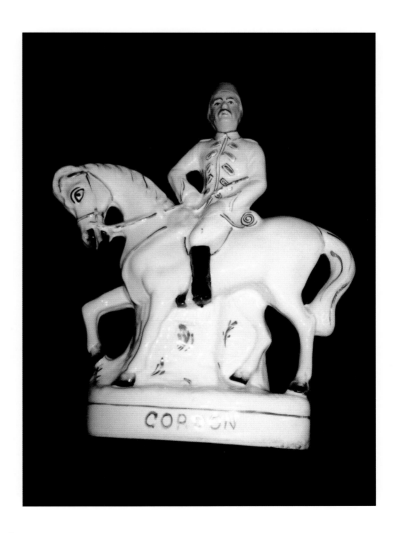

30. Haig, Sir Douglas. (1861-1928)

Known as 'Butcher' Haig, he was a disgrace to the British army. He was in charge of British forces in Belgium during part of the First World War and apart from treating his soldiers as cannon fodder, he was personally responsible for confirming the death penalty on over two hundred and fifty allied soldiers, most of whom were volunteers and suffering from shell shock, including a sixteen year old. He even confirmed the death penalty on two soldiers after the armistice had been agreed and the war was effectively over. To their credit, the Australians were the only army who refused to allow their soldiers to be shot for desertion etc. Though Haig on a number of occasions tried to gain their compliance by saying that he would only use the penalty 'sparingly,' of the three hundred and six British soldiers executed only three were officers. In comparison, the Germans executed a total of twenty-five of their own men during the war.

The son of John Haig, head of the successful whisky company he was a career soldier and after Sandhurst he was commissioned into the 7th Hussars and worked his way through the ranks. It is possible that he regretted the appalling loss of life he was responsible for, as after his retirement in 1921 he devoted the rest of his life to the welfare of ex-servicemen via the Royal British Legion.

Fig. 4078S
A titled figure of Haig, seated on a tank dressed in full military uniform holding a jug.
This figure is in the form of a jug and is part of a series of twelve figures made by Wilkinson Ltd and was limited to an edition of 350.
HEIGHT: 10 inches
TITLE: PUSH AND GO
PRICE: E

31. Jellicoe, Admiral Sir John (1859-1935)

Born in Southampton, joined the Navy and served in the Egyptian War of 1882, he was one of the survivors of the collision between *Victoria* and *Camperdown* in 1893.

Played an important part in the modernisation of the Royal Navy, and as controller of the Royal Navy during the period 1908 to 1910 was a strong supporter of the new Dreadnought battleships, torpedo boats and submarines. In 1911 Churchill appointed him second in command of the British Grand Fleet. On the outbreak of the First World War he replaced Callaghan as Commander of the British Grand Fleet and directed operations at the Battle of Jutland. He was replaced by Beatty in late 1916. He became First Sea Lord until dismissed by Prime Minister Lloyd George over a disagreement about the introduction of convoys in the Battle of the Atlantic.

Fig. 4079S
A titled figure of Jellicoe seated dressed in full naval uniform holding a jug.

This figure is in the form of a jug and is part of a series of twelve figures made by Wilkinson Ltd and was limited to an edition of 350.

Two versions are illustrated, for some reason the wording on the jug has been changed, it is not known why this was done, but the second version is very rare, there is also another version that reads 'For God–Dreadnought Die Hard' it may be that the second two were trial pieces and the potters finally decided on the first version for the limited edition.

HEIGHT: 10.5 inches
TITLE: HELL FIRE JACK or DREAD-NOUGHT DRAUGHT
PRICE: E

32. Joffre, Joseph (1852-1931)

Born in Rivesaltes, at the age of eighteen joined the French Army, in 1911 he was appointed chief of staff and he rid the army of defensively minded commanders. On the outbreak of the First World War he took command of the French Army and ordered the attack on the German Army at the Marne, he was blamed for the failure to break through on the Western Front and for the great losses at Verdun he was replaced in December 1916. Remained popular with the French public and was promoted to the position of Marshall of France.

Fig. 4080S
A figure of Joffre seated dressed in full military uniform holding a shell.
This figure is in the form of a jug and is part of a series of twelve figures made by Wilkinson Ltd and was limited to an edition of 350.
HEIGHT: 10.5 INCHES
TITLE: CE QUE J'OFFRE
PRICE: E

33. Kitchener Horatio Herbert (Earl of Khartoum and Broome) (1850-1916)

Born in Kerry in Ireland he gained a commission in 1871, part of Wolseleys expedition to relieve Gordon at Khartoum, made Sirdar, which was commander in chief of the Egyptian Army in 1892. In 1898 he avenged Gordon's death by defeating the Khalifa's army at Omdurman, he became chief of staff to Lord Roberts during the Boer War at the end of which he was created a Viscount. Became a Field Marshal in 1909, and Secretary of State for war in 1914. Famous for the poster of him which had the caption 'Your Country Needs You' entreating men to join the armed forces for the First World War, over 3.000.000 men volunteered in the first two years of the war. The Prime Minister sent him to Russia in an attempt to rally that country in its fight against Germany, he was drowned when the ship carrying him there sunk on striking a mine.

Fig. 4081S
A titled figure of Kitchener seated dressed in full military uniform holding a jug.
This figure is in the form of a jug and is part of a series of twelve figures made by Wilkinson Ltd and was issued in a limited edition.
HEIGHT: 10 inches
TITLE: BITTER FOR THE KAISER
PRICE: E

Fig. 4083A standing figure of Kitchener, titled in gilt capitals, dressed in military uniform of belted jacket with sash and medals, trousers and knee boots, holding a sword in his left hand and a scroll in his right.
HEIGHT: 14 inches
TITLE: KITCHENER
PRICE: F

Fig. 4082P
A figure of Kitchener, titled in gilt capitals, standing in front of drapery, dressed in full military uniform of peaked cap, belted jacket, trousers, and gaiters, holding a sword in his left hand, his right is on his hip holding a scroll.
This figure pairs with Roberts, (See figure 4099).
HEIGHT: 14 inches
TITLE: KITCHENER
PRICE: F

Fig. 4084P
(Not Illustrated) A titled figure of Kitchener mounted on horse-back, dressed in topee hat, military jacket and puttees, his right hand holding the reins, his left is on the horse's flank, a sword hanging from his belt.
This figure pairs with MacDonald, (See figure 4091).
This is a very rare figure made by Sampson Smith, and whilst not illustrated it is virtually a mirror image of its pair McDonald (See figure 4091). This is the only figure titled 'The Sirdar' and dates it to the Battle of Omdurman, as this was the title given to the British Commander-in-chief of the Egyptian army which position Kitchener occupied at that time.
This figure is part of a series of ten figures made by Sampson Smith all of which are very rare. The series consists of a pair of figures titled '21ˢᵗ Lancers, Buller, (See figure 4038), Kitchener, (See figures 4084, 4085), McDonald, (See figures 4091, 4092), Dundonald, (See figure 4048), Roberts, (See figure 4100) and French, (See figure 4061).
HEIGHT: 11 inches
TITLE: THE SIRDAR
PRICE: F

Fig. 4085P

(Not Illustrated) A titled figure of Kitchener, mounted on horse-back, facing left, dressed in military uniform of helmet, belted jacket, trousers and knee boots, holding the reins in his right hand, his left is on the horses flank.

This figure pairs with Roberts, (See figure 4100).

This figure is part of a series of ten figures made by Sampson Smith all of which are very rare, and whilst not illustrated it is virtually a mirror image of its pair Roberts, (See figure 4100). The series consists of a pair of figures titled '21ˢᵗ Lancers, Buller, (See figure 4038), Kitchener, (See figures 4084, 4085), McDonald, (See figures 4091, 4092), Dundonald, (See figure 4048), Roberts, (See figure 4100) and French, (See figure 4061).

HEIGHT: 11 inches
TITLE: LORD KITCHENER
PRICE: F

Fig. 4087P

(Not Illustrated) A titled figure of Kitchener, mounted on horse-back, facing left, dressed in military uniform of helmet, long jacket with sash, trousers and knee boots, his right hand holding a scroll on the horse's neck, his left resting on his thigh.

This figure pairs with French, (See figure 4062).

Whilst not illustrated this is the same figure as Buller, (See figure 4040), the only differences being a change of heads and the title.

There are a further five figures in this series which were all made by Sampson Smith to commemorate the commanders in the Boer War, they are usually found in the white but can be found coloured. The complete series consists of Buller, (See figure 4040), Roberts, (See figure 4102), Dundonald, (See figure 4049), McDonald, (See figure 4094), Kitchener, (See figure 4087) and French, (See figure 4062).

HEIGHT: 14.5 inches
TITLE: LORD KITCHENER
PRICE: F

Fig. 4086P

A titled figure of Kitchener, mounted on horseback, dressed in military uniform of fez, belted jacket, trousers and knee boots, his left hand resting on the horse's neck, his right on its flank.

This figure pairs with MacDonald, (See figure 4093).

This figure is part of a series of eight made by the Kent-Parr factory, the first pair Wolseley, (See figure 4111) and Gordon, (See figure 4077) in 1898 to commemorate Wolseley's attempt to relieve Gordon at Khartoum. The second pair Kitchener, (See figure 4086) and McDonald, (See figure 4093) to commemorate the Battle of Omdurman in 1898. The final two pairs were made in 1898/1900 to commemorate battles in the Boer War, they were figures of French, (See figure 4064), Roberts, (See figure 4101), Baden-Powell, (See figure 4031) and Buller, (See figure 4039).

HEIGHT: 15 inches
TITLE: KITCHENER
PRICE: F

Fig. 4088P

A figure of Kitchener, titled in raised capitals on a plaque, mounted on horseback, dressed in military uniform of peaked cap, belted jacket with sash and trousers, his right hand is on the horses flank, his left across his waist.

This figure pairs with French, (See figure 4063).

There are a further five figures in this series, they can all be identified by the method of applying the title via a plaque with 'v' ends. The figures are French, (See figure 4063), McDonald, (See figure 4095), Baden-Powell, (See figure 4033), Roberts, (See figure 4103) and Buller, (See figure 4041).

These figures can be found made by either the press or slip mould methods, press mould figures have been found with a factory mark 'SADLER/BURSLEM/ENGLAND.'

HEIGHT: 12 inches
TITLE: LORD KITCHENER
PRICE: F

34. Lloyd, George David (1863-1945)

The son of a headmaster, at the age of sixteen he went to work in a solicitor's office, in 1890 he was elected to parliament as a Liberal and stayed a member for Caernavon in Wales for fifty-five years. In 1906 he was appointed as president of the Board of Trade and in 1908 he became Chancellor of the Exchequer. When the First World War started in 1914 the then Prime Minister Asquith appointed Lloyd George as minister of munitions. Responsible for the reorganisation of British factories to ensure a sufficient supply of shells and guns for the forces, a subsequent disagreement with Asquith led to his resignation, but by 1916 he had become Prime Minister, putting forward the proposal that instead of each country having a separate commander there should be one overall commander for all the allied armies. In 1918 the British armies agreed to serve under the French Marshal Foch.

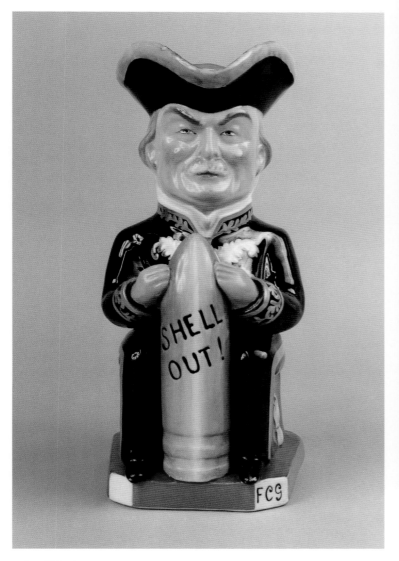

Fig. 4089S
A titled figure of Lloyd George, seated, wearing a military dress uniform and holding a large shell between his legs.
This figure is in the form of a jug and is part of a series of twelve figures made by Wilkinson Ltd and was limited to an edition of 350.
HEIGHT: 10 inches
TITLE: SHELL OUT!
PRICE: E

35. McCracken, Henry Joy (1767-1798)

An Irish patriot he was part of the United Irishmen society founded in 1791, commanded the rebels in an uprising against the English in County Antrim, in 1798 was captured tried and executed.

Fig. 4090S
A figure of McCracken titled in gilt script, standing, dressed in coat, breeches and stockings, his right hand holding his lapel, his left resting on a pedestal which is inscribed WHO FEARS TO SPEAK OF 98 - 1798/1898.
This figure is in a series of three with Wolfe Tone (See figure 4107) and Lord Edward Fitzgerald (See figure 4058).
HEIGHT: 14 inches
TITLE: HENRY JOY MCCRACKEN
PRICE: E

36. Macdonald, Sir Hector Archibald (1853-1903)

Joined the army as a private soldier and rose through the ranks to become a major-general, at seventeen he was with the Gordon Highlanders and fought in the Afghan War of 1879-1880 during which he was promoted from the ranks to second lieutenant. He fought in the Nile Expedition of 1885 and the Sudan campaign of 1888. In the Boer War he organised the relief of Kimberley; accused of 'conduct unbecoming a gentleman' and rather than face disgrace shot himself.

Fig. 4091P
(Not Illustrated) A titled figure of Macdonald, mounted on horseback, facing to the right, wearing a topee hat, belted jacket with a sash, kilt and puttees, his left hand holding the horse's reins, his right is on the horses flank.
This figure pairs with Kitchener, (See figure 4084).
This figure is part of a series of ten figures made by Sampson Smith all of which are very rare, and whilst not illustrated it is virtually a mirror image of its pair Kitchener, (See figure 4084).
The series consists of a pair of figures titled '21ˢᵗ Lancers, Buller, (See figure 4038), Kitchener, (See figures 4084, 4085, Macdonald, (See figures 4091, 4092), Dundonald, (See figure 4048), Roberts, (See figure 4100) and French, (See figure 4061).
HEIGHT: 11 inches
TITLE: COL. MACDONALD
PRICE: F

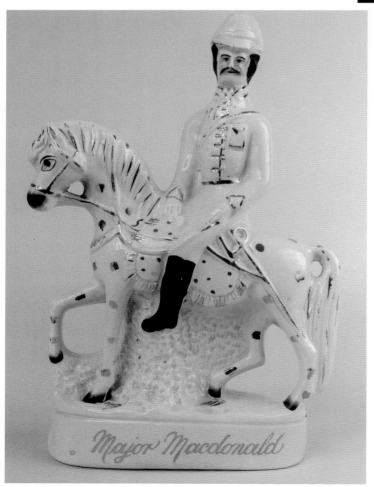

Fig. 4093P
A figure of Macdonald titled in black capitals, mounted on horseback, wearing a cocked hat belted jacket with a sash, trousers and knee boots, his left hand resting on his thigh, his right on his hip.
This figure pairs with Kitchener, (See figure 4086).
This figure is part of a series of eight made by the Kent-Parr factory, the first pair Wolseley, (See figure 4111), and Gordon, (See figure 4077) in 1898 to commemorate Wolseley's attempt to relieve Gordon at Khartoum. The second pair Kitchener, (See figure 4086), and Macdonald, (See figure 4093) to commemorate the Battle of Omdurman in 1898. The final two pairs were made in 1898/1900 to commemorate battles in the Boer War, they were figures of French, (See figure 4064), Roberts, (See figure 4101), Baden-Powell, (See figure 4031), and Buller, (See figure 4039).
HEIGHT: 15 inches
TITLE: MACDONALD
PRICE: F

Fig. 4092P
A figure of Macdonald titled in gilt script, mounted on horseback, wearing a topee hat, belted jacket with a sash, trousers and knee boots, his left hand holding the horse's reins, his right is on the horse's neck.
This figure was produced at the time of the Boer War, as distinct from Figure 4091 which was produced at the time of the battle of Omdurman. In this instance the title of Major is an abbreviation of 'Major General' to which rank he was promoted in 1900.
This figure pairs with Buller, (See figure 4038) and is identical to French, (See figure 4061) other than titling.
This figure is part of a series of ten figures made by Sampson Smith all of which are very rare. The series consists of a pair of figures titled '21ˢᵗ Lancers, Buller, (See figure 4038), Kitchener, (See figures 4084, 4085), Macdonald, (See figures 4091, 4092), Dundonald, (See figure 4048), Roberts, (See figure 4100) and French, (See figure 4061).
HEIGHT: 11.5 inches
TITLE: MAJOR MACDONALD
PRICE: F

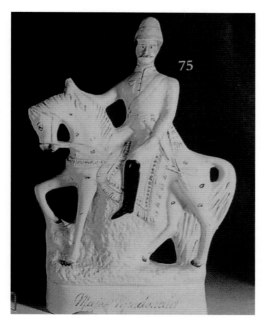

Fig. 4094P

A figure of Macdonald, titled in gilt script, mounted on horseback, wearing a helmet, belted jacket with a sash, trousers and knee boots, his left hand resting on his thigh, his right on the horse's neck.
This figure pairs with Dundonald, (See figure 4049).
This figure has been derived from the Duke of Connaught, (See figure 4050), slight changes have been made to the head and the title has been changed.
There are a further five figures in this series which were all made by Sampson Smith to commemorate the commanders in the Boer War, they are usually found in the white but can be found coloured. The complete series consists of Buller, (See figure 4040), Roberts, (See figure 4102), Dundonald, (See figure 4049), Macdonald, (See figure 4094), Kitchener, (See figure 4087) and French, (See figure 4062).
HEIGHT: 14.5 inches
TITLE: MAJOR MACDONALD
PRICE: F

Fig. 4095P

A figure of Macdonald, titled in raised capitals on a plaque, mounted on horseback, wearing a busby, and military uniform, his left hand resting on his thigh, his right to his waist.
This figure pairs with Baden-Powell Figure, (See figure 4033).
There are a further five figures in this series, they can all be identified by the method of applying the title via a plaque with 'v' ends. The figures are French, (See figure 4063), Kitchener, (See figure 4088), Baden-Powell, (See figure 4033), Roberts, (See figure 4103) and Buller, (See figure 4041).
These figures can be found made by either the press or slip mould methods, press mould figures have been found with a factory mark 'SADLER/BURSLEM/ENGLAND.'
HEIGHT: 12.5 inches
TITLE: HECTOR MACDONALD
PRICE: F

37. Nelson, Horatio (Viscount Nelson, Duke of Bronte) (1758-1805)

Born at Burnham Thorpe, Norfolk on the 29th September, his father being the rector of the parish. Not much is known of his early childhood apart from his schooling at Norwich. He entered the Royal Navy in 1771 as a midshipman, soon joining his uncle on the Triumph as a 'captain's servant.' In 1773 at his request he was transferred to the Carcass, a voyage of discovery in the Artic. Returning, he joined the *Seahorse*, a frigate and toured the East Indies, but due to the climate his health failed and he was relieved and on the 14th March 1776 he returned to England. A few weeks after his return he was appointed lieutenant of the Worcester under the command of Captain Mark Robinson. In 1777, Nelson was again promoted to lieutenant of the *Lowestoft* under the command of William Locker, learning many valuable lessons from him. In 1778 he was appointed captain of a captured French ship, which was renamed *Hinchinbroke* and led an expedition against Grenada, but infected with malaria he returned to Jamaica and then to England. In 1783 after various duties he was appointed to the *Boreas* where he sailed to the West Indies and proceeded to capture five American ships engaged in illegal trading. Proceedings for illegal detention were served on Nelson and he was forced to be a prisoner on his ship. Eventually an order came through, and the Crown agreed to defend their captain at any cost. In March of 1783 he sailed to St. Kitts, on his arrival he met and fell in love with the young widow Frances Nisbet and in March of 1787 he married and returned home. In 1793 with the outbreak of war with France looming, Nelson was given command of the *Agememnon* where he sailed to Naples and there met Emma Hamilton, the wife of Sir William Hamilton the English minister, and began an affair which would continue until his death. In 1796 he was appointed rear-admiral and in 1797 after an unsuccessful landing at Santa Cruz he was injured and had to have his right arm amputated. In 1798 he attacked the French fleet in Aboukir Bay where he lost the sight in one eye, and was created Baron Nelson of the Nile. Returning to England in 1801 in the company of the Hamilton's, he separated from his wife and lived with the Hamilton's in London. William Hamilton died in 1803 and in the following years until Nelson's death Nelson and Emma lived together and Emma bore him children.

In May of 1803 he was appointed commander-in-chief of the Mediterranean fleet and made the *Victory* his flagship. He set off to do battle with the French fleet and after chasing Villeneuve, the commander-in-chief of the French fleet, to the West Indies and back, they met at Cape Trafalgar. The English victory was complete and decisive and the outcome decided when Nelson was shot on his quarterdeck from the *Redoubtable* at a range of fifteen yards and within the hour he was dead. His body was brought back to England where after laying in state at Greenwich he was publicly buried at St. Paul's Cathedral on the 6th January 1806. Of all the monuments erected to his memory, the most famous is the column in Trafalgar Square, London.

Fig. 4096
A standing figure of Nelson titled in black script, dressed in Navy uniform of tri-corn hat, jacket with epaulettes, waistcoat, breeches with shoes, his right sleeve is pinned to his waistcoat and his left at his side holding a telescope.
This figure is made in the form of a jug, a large handle protrudes from the back, it can be found listed in the Kent catalogue under Toby Jugs Nelson Ref. 372.
The figure illustrated dates from about 1910 and continued to be made for many years, what is unusual is that underglaze blue was used on his jacket, underglaze colours were not in general use after approximately 1865 and the Parr-Kent factory rarely used them at all.
HEIGHT: 11.5 inches
TITLE: NELSON
PRICE: F

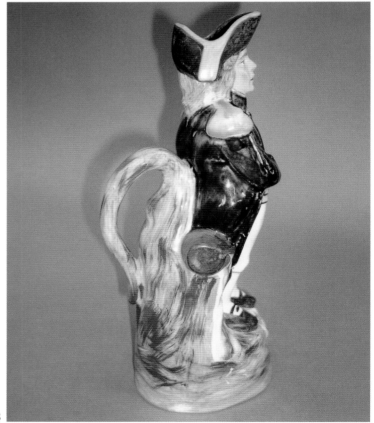

38. Parnell, Charles Stewart (1846-1891)

An Irish patriot and politician, stood and was elected as a Home Rule candidate for Meath in 1875, and used his position as a Member of Parliament to cause disruption and obstruction, he was elected as president of the Irish National Land League and as such came into confrontation with Gladstone the Prime Minister, he refused to accept the will of Parliament on Gladstone's Land Bill and Gladstone imprisoned him in Kilmainham jail, after his release he negotiated with Gladstone the 'Kilmainham treaty'. Falsely accused of crimes in a bid to discredit him but a Royal Commission vindicated him and he received substantial damages. His career was subsequently ruined by having a sexual affair with the wife of a Captain O'Shea, a divorce decree was granted to the Captain, and costs awarded against Parnell. He retired from public life and married the former Mrs. O'Shea, but died shortly thereafter.

Fig. 4097P
A figure of Parnell titled in raised capitals, standing, dressed incongruously in a Greek dress holding a shillelagh in his left hand and a large flag with the Union Jack with an Irish Harp depicted on it in his right.
This figure pairs with Gladstone, (See figure 4072).
This figure and its pair were made to commemorate the Kilmainham Peace Treaty of 1882, between England and Ireland, a centrepiece for his pair was also made of an Angel standing above and behind two women representing Britannia and Ireland, (See figure 4120) which figure was remodelled in 1902 to commemorate the ending of the Boer War.
HEIGHT: 13.75 inches
TITLE: C. S. PARNELL
PRICE: E

39. Roberts, Evan (1878-1951)

A Welsh revivalist the son of a miner who also worked in the mines himself, he left the mines and attended a school for ministers. After leaving he started a revivalist movement which attracted enormous audiences. His private life and morals were questioned and this led to his early retirement.

Fig. 4098
A figure of Roberts, titled in gilt capitals, standing, dressed in frock coat, waistcoat and trousers his left hand resting on a pillar and his right is held aloft.
This is a particularly rare figure; not more than two examples have been recorded and it can be dated to circa 1905 when the great religious revival in Wales took place, but for this fact the figure could have been assumed to have been made Circa 1870 as its style is Victorian, it is one of the few new personalities potted in the 20th century.
HEIGHT: 13.5 inches
TITLE: EVAN ROBERTS
PRICE: With portrait figures of this rarity it is price by negotiation, the last time an example was offered for sale in 2002 it was priced at £1400.

40. Roberts, Frederick Sleigh, (Earl of Kandahar, Pretoria and Waterford) (1832-1914)

Born in India he attended Sandhurst. He first saw action during the Indian Mutiny in 1857, in 1858 during the same campaign he won the Victoria Cross, the highest military award. He served with Lord Napier during the Abyssinian expedition and later conducted the march from Kabul to Kandahar which resulted in the pacification of Afghanistan, he was made a Baron in 1892 and a Field-marshal in 1895, served with distinction during the Boer War. He was created an Earl for his services there, he died whilst serving in France during the First World War at the age of 82!

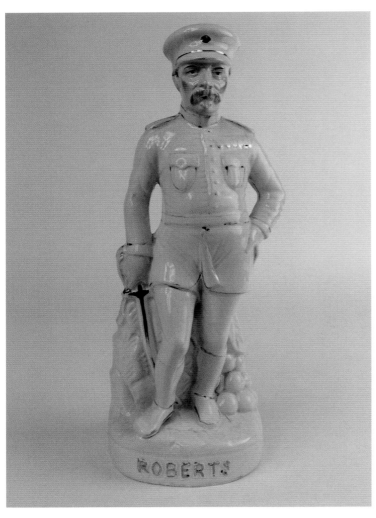

Fig. 4099P
A standing figure of Roberts, titled in raised gilt capitals, dressed in military uniform of peaked cap, jacket and trousers with leggings, he holds a sword in his right hand and his left is on his hip; there is a pile of cannon balls at his feet.
This figure pairs with Kitchener, (See figure 4082).
HEIGHT: 14 inches
TITLE: ROBERTS
PRICE: F

Fig. 4100P
A mounted figure of Roberts titled in gilt script, dressed in military uniform of cocked hat, jacket and trousers with knee boots, holding the reins in his left hand, his right resting on the horse's flank.
This figure pairs with Kitchener, (See figure 4085).
This figure is part of a series of ten figures made by Sampson Smith all of which are very rare. The series consists of a pair of figures titled '21ˢᵗ Lancers, Buller, (See figure 4038), Kitchener, (See figures 4084, 4085), McDonald, (See figures 4091, 4092), Dundonald, (See figure 4048), Roberts, (See figure 4100) and French, (See figure 4061).
This figure is identical to Dundonald, (See figure 4048) other than titling.
Two figures are illustrated, and one has been mis-titled 'Major Macdonald;' this is not unique in this series, as a figure of 'The Sirdar' (See figure 4084) has been seen mis-titled 'Lord Roberts.'
HEIGHT: 11 inches
TITLE: LORD ROBERTS
PRICE: F

Fig. 4101P
A figure of Roberts titled in gilt capitals, mounted on horseback, dressed in military uniform of cocked hat, jacket and trousers with knee boots, holding the reins in his right hand, his left is on his thigh.
This figure pairs with French, (See figure 4064).
This figure is part of a series of eight made by the Kent-Parr factory, the first pair Wolseley, (See figure 4111) and Gordon, (See figure 4077) in 1898 to commemorate Wolseley's attempt to relieve Gordon at Khartoum. The second pair Kitchener, (See figure 4086) and McDonald, (See figure 4093), to commemorate the Battle of Omdurman in 1898. The final two pairs were made in 1898/1900 to commemorate battles in the Boer War, they were figures of French, (See figure 4064), Roberts, (See figure 4101), Baden-Powell, (See figure 4031) and Buller, (See figure 4039).
HEIGHT: 14.5 inches
TITLE: ROBERTS.
PRICE: F

Fig. 4102P

A figure of Roberts, titled in gilt script, mounted on horseback, dressed in military uniform of helmet, jacket and breeches with knee boots, his right hand resting on his thigh, his left holding a scroll on the horse's neck.

This figure pairs with Buller, (See figure 4040).

This figure can also be found titled Lord Roberts, he was created a Baron in 1892 so therefore figures titled thus, must be after that date.

This figure is exactly the same figure as French, (See figure 4062), the only difference being the title.

There are a further five figures in this series which were all made by Sampson Smith to commemorate the commanders in the Boer war, they are usually found in the white but can be found coloured. The complete series consists of Buller, (See figure 4040), Roberts, (See figure 4102), Dundonald, (See figure 4049), McDonald, (See figure 4094), Kitchener, (See figure 4087) and French, (See figure 4062).

HEIGHT: 14.5 inches
TITLE: GENERAL ROBERTS
PRICE: F

Fig. 4103P

A figure of Roberts, titled in raised capitals on a plaque, mounted on horseback, dressed in military uniform of plumed helmet, jacket and breeches with knee boots, his left hand resting on his thigh, his right holding the reins.

This figure pairs with Buller, (See figure 4041).

There are a further five figures in this series, they can all be identified by the method of applying the title via a plaque with 'v' ends. The figures are French, (See figure 4063), McDonald, (See figure 4095), Baden-Powell, (See figure 4033), Kitchener, (See figure 4088) and Buller, (See figure 4041).

These figures can be found made by either the press or slip mould methods, press mould figures have been found with a factory mark 'SADLER/BURSLEM/ENGLAND.'

HEIGHT: 12.25 inches
TITLE: LORD ROBERTS
PRICE: F

41. Sarsfield, Patrick (Earl of Lucan) (1645–1693)

An Irish patriot, educated at a French military college, he was the Lieutenant-colonel of Dover's horse in 1685 when he received from King James II the command of all the Irish troops in England at which time he was created an Earl, taking the title Earl of Lucan as he had been born in Lucan. Escaping with the King to France and then to Ireland, driving the English out of Sligo and was present at the battle of the Boyne in 1690. He defended Limerick and when it fell to the English he once again escaped to France joining the French army along with many of his troops. He was in command of the Irish soldiers intended for the invasion of England and fought at Steenkirk in 1692. He was killed at Neerwinden, near Landen in 1693.

42. Sexton, Thomas (1848-1932)

Irish politician and a follower of Parnell, he was imprisoned at Kilmainham jail with him. Like Parnell, he used his position in Parliament obstructively; he introduced a bill into Parliament to remove a Nelson's column which had been erected in the centre of Dublin and which was objected to in Republican circles, the bill was defeated, later falling out with Parnell, standing and successful as an anti-Parnell member of Parliament for North Kerry from 1892 to 1896.

Fig. 4104
A figure of a Sarsfield, titled in gilt script, mounted on horseback, dressed in military uniform of tri-corn hat, jacket with epaulettes and belt across his chest and waist, breeches and knee boots, his left hand is by a sword which is hanging from his waist, his right resting on the horse's neck holding a scroll. **This is not a true portrait of Sarsfield. The potters serving two markets, Protestant and Catholic, titled figures of King William III, 'Sarsfield' thus able to sell to both sides of the religious divide; other figures of William have also been recorded so titled.**
TITLE: SARSFIELD
HEIGHT: 12.75 inches
PRICE: F

Fig. 4105
A figure of Sexton standing in front of brickwork, bareheaded and bearded, dressed in frock coat, large knotted tie and trousers, his right hand is across his chest and his left resting on a pillar to his side.
HEIGHT: 15.5 inches
PRICE: F

43. Stewart, Sir Herbert (1843-1885)

The Brigade-Major of cavalry in the Zulu War of 1879, becoming Wolseley's military secretary in 1880, he was awarded a knighthood following the Suakim campaign of 1884, killed in action when in command of the desert column attempting the relief of General Gordon.

Fig. 4106P
A figure of Stewart titled in raised capital, mounted on horseback, dressed in military uniform of helmet jacket with sash, breeches and knee boots, his left hand resting on the horses mane holding the reins, his right on his thigh holding a sword.
This figure pairs with Burnaby, (See figure 4043).
This figure and its pair were memorial figures as both Stewart and Burnaby died of their wounds incurred in the campaign to relieve Gordon at Khartoum.
HEIGHT: 14.5 inches
TITLE: G. STEWART
PRICE: F

44. Tone, Theobald Wolfe (1763-1798)

An Irish patriot and nationalist, born in Dublin, became a lawyer and practised in Ireland, he helped organise and became an officer in United Irishmen, whose main aim was to secure independence for Ireland. Due to his activities he was forced to leave Ireland and went to the United States. He left after two years and went to France where he agitated and was successful in joining and becoming an officer in a French squadron which attempted to invade Ireland. A battle ensued and Tone was captured and sentenced to be hung as a traitor; before the sentence could be carried out he committed suicide by cutting his throat in prison.

Fig. 4107S
A figure of Tone, titled in gilt script, standing, dressed in a military coat with sword, breeches and stockings, his right hand resting on his thigh, his left holding two crossed flags against his chest, there is a pedestal to his right which is inscribed WHO FEARS TO SPEAK OF 98 - 1798/1898.
This figure along with McCracken (See figure 4090) and Fitzgerald (See figure 4059) were produced in 1898, 100 years after the event to commemorative the deaths of these three Irish patriots in the abortive uprising of 1798.
This figure is in a series of three with McCracken (See figure 4090) and Fitzgerald, (See figure 4058).
HEIGHT: 14 inches
TITLE: THEOBALD WOLFE TONE
PRICE: E

45. Wilson, Thomas Woodrow (1856-1924)

Born in Staunton, Virginia and educated at Princeton, the University of Virginia and John Hopkins University, he was a professor at Princeton from 1890 to 1902. Elected Democratic Governor of New Jersey in 1911 and became a national figure due to his progressive views on reform. In 1912 he was elected the 28th President of the United States. On the outbreak of the First World War he declared a policy of strict neutrality, opinion against Germany hardened with the sinking of the Lusitania and the pacifist Secretary of State resigned to be replaced by the pro-allied Robert Lansing. The tide of opinion eventually turned against Germany due in part to the publication of the Zimmerman telegram that suggested that Germany was willing to help Mexico regain territory in Texas and Arizona. In April 1917, Wilson asked permission to go to war and this was approved in the Senate by 82 votes to 6 and two days later by the House of Representatives by 373 to 50.

46. Wolseley, Garnet Joseph (Viscount) (1833-1913)

Born in Dublin of an English family, he joined the army at the age of nineteen and served in the Crimean War of 1854–1856, the Indian mutiny of 1857-1859 and the China War of 1860. For his services during the Red River Expedition of 1870 he was awarded a KCMG. Commander in chief of the expedition which suppressed the rebellion of the Egyptian army and subsequently occupied Cairo, for this action he was created a Baron, he attempted the relief of General Gordon in 1885 and was created a Viscount, became a Field Marshal and Commander in chief of the British Army in 1895.

Fig. 4108S
A figure of Wilson seated dressed in hat, coat and striped trousers holding a Bi-plane.
This figure is in the form of a jug and is part of a series of twelve figures made by Wilkinson Ltd. and was limited to an edition of 500.
HEIGHT: 10 inches
TITLE: WELCOME UNCLE SAM
PRICE: E

Fig. 4109P
A figure of Wolseley titled in raised capitals, mounted on horseback, in military uniform of helmet, cross belted jacket with a sash, trousers and knee boots, his right hand resting on his thigh, his left on the horse's neck.
This figure pairs with Duke of Connaught, (See figure 4050).
HEIGHT: 14.25 inches
TITLE: G. WOLSELEY
PRICE: F

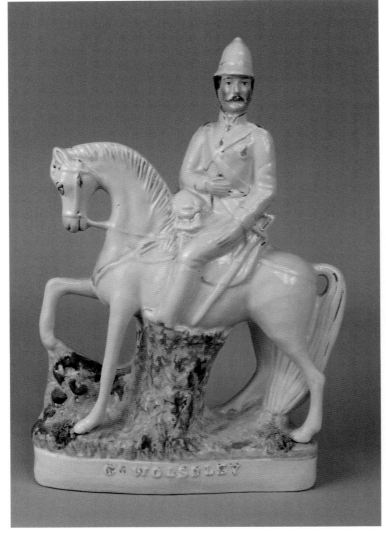

Fig. 4110P
A figure of Wolseley titled in raised capitals, mounted on horseback, in military uniform of helmet, cross belted jacket with a sash, trousers and knee boots, his left hand resting on his thigh, his right holding the reins, a sword hanging from his belt.
This figure pairs with Duke of Connaught, (See figure 4051).
This and its pair the Duke of Connaught are very rare figures.
HEIGHT: 12.5 inches
TITLE: G. WOLSELEY
PRICE: E

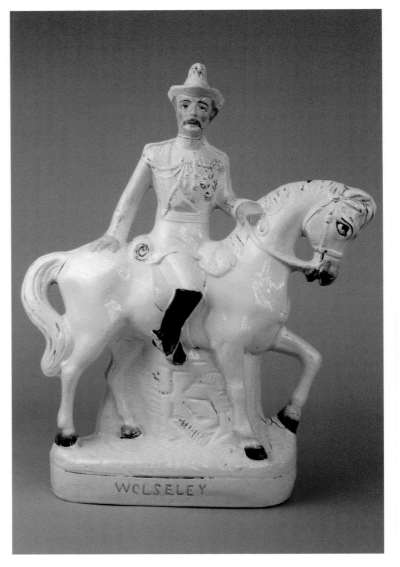

Fig. 4111P
A figure of Wolseley titled in raised capitals, mounted on horseback, dressed in military uniform of cocked hat, jacket with a sash, breeches and knee boots, his left hand holding the reins and his right resting on the horses flank.
This figure pairs with Gordon, (See figure 4077).
This figure is part of a series of eight made by the Kent-Parr factory, the first pair Wolseley, (See figure 4111), and Gordon, (See figure 4077) in 1898 to commemorate Wolseley's attempt to relieve Gordon at Khartoum. The second pair Kitchener, (See figure 4086) and McDonald, (See figure 4093) to commemorate the Battle of Omdurman in 1898. The final two pairs were made in 1898/1900 to commemorate battles in the Boer War, they were figures of French, (See figure 4064), Roberts, (See figure 4101), Baden-Powell, (See figure 4031) and Buller, (See figure 4039).
HEIGHT: 15 inches
TITLE: G. WOLSELEY
PRICE: F

Chapter 2: Decorative and Other Figures

Many of the figures still being produced after 1875 were from moulds that had been used before, and many of these figures are not included in this book. Original versions will be found in the companion volumes 'Victorian Staffordshire Figures 1835-1875.

We have however, included a selection of these later figures, including some portrait figures. As these figures were made many years after the person had died or had faded into history, these were by this time being made as decorative figures and they have been treated as such. Alongside each of these figures a reference number as it appears in the companion volumes is listed.

The post 1875 figures are relatively easy to identify, **'bright gold'** is applied which is as the name suggests a much brighter and more brassy colouring than the **'best gold'** which was used up to about 1875. Also the use of underglaze blue ceased almost entirely, many of the figures produced did not have very much enamel colouring, the decorators relying on just flesh tones for face and hands, and overglaze black for highlighting the detail.

In comparison to the earlier period, few new master moulds were made. It does appear that as the trade declined many of these and earlier moulds found their way into the hands of just a few potters.

On a few of these figures a registration number does appear; this will date a figure accurately to the first year the design was registered.

From 1842 until 1883 a diamond registration design was used with a 'bubble' above, in which the class of goods was noted, i.e. class 111 was for glass items. After this date, from 1884 onwards, all classes were amalgamated, the numbering started at 1, along with Rd, (Registration No.).

Up until the outbreak of the first world war, on average, just over 20,000 new designs were registered each year, the war years saw a falling off in new designs registered, but by 1955, 876067 new designs were registered. For dating purposes, the year and number registered is listed below.

1884	1	**1885**	19754	**1886**	40480
1887	64520	**1888**	90483	**1889**	116648
1890	141273	**1891**	163767	**1892**	185713
1893	205240	**1894**	224720	**1895**	246975
1896	268392	**1897**	291241	**1898**	311658
1899	331707	**1900**	351202	**1901**	368154
1902	385088	**1903**	402913	**1904**	424017
1905	447548	**1906**	471486	**1907**	493487
1908	518415	**1909**	534963	**1910**	552000
1911	574817	**1912**	594195	**1913**	612431
1914	630190	**1915**	644935	**1916**	653521
1917	658988	**1918**	662872	**1919**	666128
1920	673750	**1921**	680147	**1922**	687144
1923	694907	**1924**	702671	**1925**	710165
1926	718057	**1927**	726330	**1928**	734370
1929	742725	**1930**	751160	**1931**	760583
1932	769670	**1933**	779292	**1934**	789019
1935	799097	**1936**	808794	**1937**	812793
1938	825231	**1939**	832610	**1940**	837520
1941	838590	**1942**	839230	**1943**	839980
1944	841040	**1945**	842670	**1946**	845550
1947	849730	**1948**	853260	**1949**	856999
1950	860854	**1951**	863970	**1952**	866635
1953	869300	**1954**	872531	**1955**	876067

Figs. 4112/4113
A pair of equestrian figures of soldiers with cocked hats, dressed in military uniform.
The Top figure is an adaptation of a portrait figure of Marshal MacMahon (See V.S.F 1835-1875, figure 192); small alterations have been made to the mould, such as a reduction in the size of his epaulettes.
MacMahon pairs with a figure of William King of Prussia, and this pair was made in 1870, as both were commanders in the Franco-Prussian War.
However the figure of the King of Prussia is different from MacMahon and it would appear that a mirror image pair has been made at a later date.
HEIGHT: 11 inches
PRICE: Pair F, Singles G

Figs. 4114/4115
A pair of figures of Hussars, mounted on horseback, they are mirror images of each other, the Hussar seated astride, holding the reins, dressed in full uniform.

These figures are more usually found in the white, and were first made by the Kent factory, Circa 1900. These are non-portrait Boer War figures, the factory continued to produce them for many years and they were still listed in the Kent price list for 1955.

A single left hand side figure and a pair that are the finest examples the authors have seen are illustrated.
HEIGHT: 10 inches
PRICE: Pair F, Singles G

Fig. 4116
A figure of a soldier and sailor standing arm in arm, the soldier on the left wearing a lancers cap, greatcoat, tunic, trousers and knee boots, carrying a bag under his right arm. The sailor on the right wearing a hat, open jacket, shirt and bell bottoms, carrying a bundle in his left hand.
Two figures illustrated identical apart from colouring.
This figure is of a British sailor and 21st Lancer who fought together in the River War of 1898.
HEIGHT: 12 inches
PRICE: F

Figs. 4117/4118
A titled pair of figures of mounted Lancers each sitting astride their horse, dressed in Lancers military uniform. These figures are virtual mirror images of each other.
Bottom figure (Figure 4118) only illustrated.
TITLE: 21st Lancers
HEIGHT: 11 inches
PRICE: Pair F, Singles F

The 21st Lancers

The 21st Lancers were renowned for their charge at the Battle of Omdurman in 1898. It was probably the last cavalry charge and was hardly a success, over three hundred officers and men found themselves in a ravine facing several thousand Dervishes who were standing twenty to thirty deep. Instead of retreating they charged straight at the solid mass, on regrouping at the end of the charge they found they had lost seventy-four dead and over a third of their horses killed.

Winston Churchill, a twenty-four year old lieutenant was at the time attached to the Lancers, but due to an injury he was unable to hold a lance. He managed however to shoot his way clear, and in his memoir's he wrote that 'it was the most dangerous two minutes I shall live to see.'

Fig. 4120

A group figure of two women seated, one with a harp, the other with a shield, shaking hands, an angel with outstretched wings standing behind.

This figure was produced to commemorate the Kilmainham Peace Treaty of 1882 between England and Ireland, the woman on the left representing Ireland and the woman on the right Britannia, this is the centrepiece for the pair of Parnell (See figure 4097) and Gladstone, (See figure 4072).

This figure was remodelled in 1902 to commemorate the ending of the Boer War (See figure 4119).

HEIGHT: 12 inches

PRICE: E

Fig. 4119

A titled group figure of two men seated shaking hands, an angel with outstretched wings stands behind and over them.

This figure is an adaptation of figure 4120 in which the Irishwoman and Britannia have been replaced by a Boer and John Bull. The foreground has been changed to include a rifle, the angel in Figure 4120 which is holding a snake has been altered to a banner that reads 'Peace on earth, goodwill towards men.'

This is a very rare figure, usually very sparsely coloured, and commemorates the ending of the Boer War.

HEIGHT: 12.5 inches

TITLE: BOER WAR PEACE DECLARED JUNE 1st 1902

PRICE: E

Figs. 4121/4122P
A titled pair of figures of standing highland soldiers, dressed in kilt, tunic and Busby, holding rifles with fixed bayonets in their right hands.
Both of these regiments fought with distinction during the Boer war and these figures commemorate that event.
HEIGHT: 12.5 inches
TITLE: GORDON HIGHLANDER–BLACK WATCH
PRICE: Pair F, Singles G

Fig. 4123P
A titled figure of Garibaldi standing in front of his horse, holding his sword in his left hand, his right is on the horse's neck holding the reins.
Guiseppe Garibaldi (1807 - 1882). The unifier of Italy, visited England to a fevered reception in 1864, being perceived as the hero of Italian independence.
TITLE: GARIBALDI
HEIGHT: 9 inches
PRICE: F

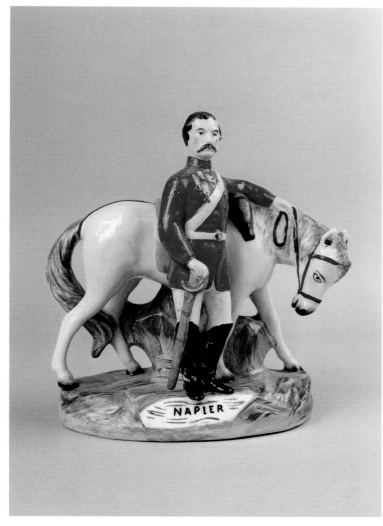

Fig. 4124P
A titled figure of Napier standing in front of his horse, holding his sword in his right hand, his left on the horse's neck holding the reins.
Robert Cornelis Napier (1810-1890) (first Baron Napier of Magdala). Appointed the command of the Abyssinian expedition in 1868, from which the figure first dates.
The Garibaldi figure was first made in 1861 and it was seven years before it was decided that a figure of Napier should be made to pair it.
TITLE: NAPIER
HEIGHT: 9 inches
PRICE: F

Figures 4123 and 4124 were first made in the 1860's (See V.S.F 1835-1875, Figures 139 & 216), and could have been included in the Portrait Chapter. It was very unusual if not exceptional for Portrait figures to be made for long periods, usually they commemorated a particular event with which the person was connected, the event, a war for example. Having passed, that person was forgotten and the potters carried on with the next personage in the news.
The above two figures proved an exception to the rule, and they must have been very popular, as they were still being made some ninety years after the event, the figures illustrated were made in the Kent factory about 1920. Most of the later figures are not titled thus suggesting that they were being sold as a pair of decorative ornaments.

Fig. 4125P
A titled equestrian figure of Napoleon, seated astride his horse, wearing a tricorn hat, jacket with epaulettes, waistcoat and breeches with boots, his right hand holding a scroll on the horse's neck, his other hand resting on his waist, below is a large clockface surrounded by grapes and leaves.
This figure was made by Sampson Smith in 1948, the mould for it was discovered amongst others in a disused part of the factory, its pair the Duke of Wellington was also made. At the time the originals were unknown and they are still extremely rare, not more than two pairs have been recorded. (See V.S.F 1835-1875, figure 20A).
It is interesting to note that on the reproductions underglaze blue has been used and that the colouring on the base is very similar to the colouring on late 19th century figures.
TITLE: NAPOLEON
HEIGHT: 16.25 inches
PRICE: E

Fig. 4129
A group figure of a seated girl and standing sailor, she wearing a blouse and long skirt and holding her hat in her right hand, he standing holding a flag in his right hand his left elbow resting on a barrel, wearing sailor attire.
This figure is similar to a number of 'Sailor's Return' figures, which first date to the Crimean War period of 1854/1856, but the author's have not seen an early version of this figure though one may exist.
HEIGHT: 8.5 inches
PRICE: G

Fig. 4130
A group figure of two sailors and a girl all seated on rockwork a waterfall below and a flag behind, the sailor on the left holding his hands in prayer, the one on the right has one hand to his chest and the other around a girl who sits between them and resting her head on his shoulder.
This figure is probably theatrical in origin and is known as 'Deliverance' as it appears to portray the rescue of either or both the girl and the sailors.
HEIGHT: 14 inches
PRICE: G

Fig. 4131
A group figure of two men seated either side of a barrel, one leaning on it the other reading a newspaper.
There is an earlier version of this quite common figure (See V.S.F 1835-1875, figure 927) the man on the right is reading a newspaper with the headline 'WAR', it was probably first produced at the time of the outbreak of the Crimean War in 1854 and remade each time a subsequent war or skirmish ensued.
HEIGHT: 9.5 inches
PRICE: G

Fig. 4141
(See. V.S.F 1835-1875, figure 1076) A figure of Romeo and Juliet seated underneath an arbour.
This was a very popular figure and was originally produced in about 1855 by the Parr factory; it was made in at least four sizes from 5 inches up to 10 inches though most of the later production was of the 7-inch size.
HEIGHT: 7 inches
PRICE: G

Fig. 4142
A group figure of Romeo & Juliet both standing with their arms clasped around each other, he wearing a jerkin and kilt, she wearing a bodice and long skirt.
This popular figure was first produced in the 1850's and the early figure will be found illustrated in Book One V.S.F 1835-1875, (Figure 1073). It was made by the Parr factory and its source was an engraving from the Tallis Shakespeare Gallery. Early figures are either titled with a quotation from the play or are not titled.
Only late figures made by Kent, as illustrated are titled 'Romeo & Juliet.
TITLE: ROMEO & JULIET
HEIGHT: 10.5 inches
PRICE: E

Fig. 4143
A figure of a man standing his left hand holding a large flag, his right across his waist, he is crowned and wearing armour, a shield is on the base between his feet.
This figure has been identified from a similar Parian figure as being of King Henry V, it was made by the Sampson Smith factory in about 1880.
There is an engraving of this figure on a page of an old Sampson Smith catalogue.
HEIGHT: 15.5 inches
PRICE: G

Fig. 4144
A seated figure of Britannia, on a square marbled base, she seated with a lion at her left side, a shield to her right on which she resting her hand, her right hand is held outstretched in which she holds a trident (missing-it was usually made of metal), she is dressed in helmet and long flowing dress.
Earlier versions of this figure do exist (See V.S.F 1835-1875, figure 3341) the one illustrated dates from about 1890.
HEIGHT: 14.5 inches
PRICE: F

Fig. 4145
(See V.S.F 1835-1875, figure 976) A group figure of Tam O'Shanter and Souter Johnny both seated holding drinking vessels with a barrel between them.
Tam O' Shanter and Souter Johnny was a poem by Robert Bu.rns.
This figure was made by Sampson Smith and can be found with a factory mark 'SAMPSON SMITH LONGTON STAFF ENGLAND 1892, the date is probably the date of manufacture. A figure has also been found with an alternative factory mark 'SAMPSON SMITH 1851 LONGTON' which date probably refers to the inception of production at Sampson Smith.
TITLE: TAM O'SHANTER AND SOUTER JOHNNY
HEIGHT: 13 inches
PRICE:G

Figs. 4146/4147
A pair of standing figures of a fisherman and wife, he standing with one foot on a basket dressed in brimmed hat, shirt and trousers a large net over both shoulders, his right arm across his waist, his left around a basket of fish which is on a brick wall beside him, she wearing a headscarf, bodice and long skirt her right arm resting on a pillar over which is draped a net, holding a basket of fish with both hands.
HEIGHT: 14 inches
PRICE: Pair F, Singles G

Fig. 4148
A figure of a bust of a man holding a basket with a dead rabbit on the top, wearing a hat decorated with vine leaves in the form of a jug. **This figure can be found in four graduating sizes, it is well modelled and decorated and if it was not for the fact that it always has bright gold on the decoration, it would in view of the use of underglaze blue be taken as being earlier than 1875.**
TITLE: MERRY CHRISTMAS
HEIGHT: 8 inches
PRICE: F

Fig. 4149
A figure of a snuff taker in the form of a jug.
This figure illustrated in the 1955 Kent catalogue as Snuff Taker No. 390.
HEIGHT: 12 inches
PRICE:G

Fig. 4150
A figure of Punch seated with legs crossed in the form of a jug.
This is also illustrated in the 1955 Kent catalogue as Punch No. 381, there should be a stopper in the form of his hat but more often than not this has been lost.
There is also a companion pair to this figure of Judy, (Figure 4151) has been reserved for it.
HEIGHT: 12 inches
PRICE: G

Fig. 4154
An arbour figure of two lovers seated, she wearing a bodice, and long skirt, he a hat, shirt, jacket and kilt, he holds her hand in his. **This figure is typical of many similar made after 1875, they are usually quite large and lack all but basic decoration, often with a large amount of bright gold gilding. Two examples are illustrated; there are slight modelling differences to the heads.**
HEIGHT: 13.75
PRICE: G

Figs. 4152/4153
A pair of figures of harvesters, she standing wearing a bodice and long dress with an apron, one foot is raised on rockwork her left arm resting on a sheaf of corn and she holds another on her head, he standing, wearing a hat, short cloak, blouse and knee breeches, his right arm resting on a sheaf of corn and another stands at his feet. **These are large well-modelled figures that were originally gilded, this has almost all disappeared.**
HEIGHT: 13.25 inches
PRICE: Pair F, Singles G

Fig. 4155
Another arbour figure of two lovers holding hands dressed similarly to the preceding pair.
It would be surprising if the same factory made two such similar figures and it is probable that Figures 4154 and 4155 originated from competing potters Sampson Smith and Lancaster.
HEIGHT: 13.5 inches
PRICE: G

Figs. 4160/4161
A pair of standing figures of goalkeepers, one has his left foot raised resting on a football, both hands on hips, dressed in shirt, shorts and boots with stockings, the other stands holding the ball in his right hand his left on his hip.
An unusual pair of figures in so far as a registration number appears on the bottom No. 866136, which dates these figures to 1951.
A similar figure to Figure 4160 appeared in a Christie's sale in 1997 it was catalogued as 'A Britannia pottery figure of 'Wee Macgregor' dressed as an Irish International player, his right foot resting on a football' It sold for over £500.
The above description is unlikely as the companion figure has the goalkeeper holding a ball in his right hand and the shirt on this figure is usually decorated with green stripes, as opposed to a blue shirt. It is believed that these two figures represent the goalkeepers for Glasgow Rangers and Glasgow Celtic football clubs.
the Britannia Pottery Co. Ltd. was in production between 1920 and 1935 and the factory was sited at St. Rollox, Glasgow in Scotland. They were previously known as Cochran and Fleming, which Company was in existence from 1896 to 1920. A director of that Company, Mr. J. Arnold Fleming wrote a book 'Scottish Pottery' but no mention of such figures appeared.
It would be interesting to know whether the figure sold bore a factory mark, as that factory had closed before these figures was made.
HEIGHT: 15 inches
PRICE: E

Fig. 4162
(See V.S.F 1835-1875 Figure 1805). A double-sided figure portraying on one side a well-dressed man holding a moneybag and on the other a poorly dressed man in ragged coat, hat and trousers holding a bottle.
This is a temperance figure promoting the benefits of drinking water as opposed to gin and was first made in the 1860's by the Parr factory, it continued to be made by Kent for many years and is illustrated in their 1955 catalogue as Novelty figure (Gin & Water) Double sided No. 258.
HEIGHT: 8.5 inches
TITLE: GIN/WATER
PRICE: F

Fig. 4163
(See V.S.F 1835-1875, figure 3384). A figure of Bacchus seated on a barrel, bearded, a garland of grapes and leaves on his head, dressed in open necked shirt and trousers, holding a tumbler of wine in his right hand, his coat draped over the barrel.
HEIGHT: 6.5 inches
PRICE: H

Fig. 4164
A standing figure of a young black boy polishing a boot, the other boot is on the base beside him, wearing a jacket and apron, breeches, stockings and shoes.
This figure was made by the Kent factory and is illustrated in their 1960 catalogue (See Plate No. 11) Where it is described as 'Shoeblack No. 345'
HEIGHT: 10.75 inches
PRICE: F

Figs. 4165/4166
(V.S.F 1835-1875, figures 2183/2184). A pair of square based figures of a cobbler and his wife, he seated with his left foot on a brick, mending a shoe dressed in cap, shirt, apron and breeches, she seated pouring water into a cup dressed in headscarf, coat and long dress.
These have been a popular pair since the early 1800's, they can be found in two sizes. The small pair illustrated are usually 20th century reproductions but 14 inch versions can be found which are mid to late 19th century. They are referred to in the Kent list as 'Jobson and Nell (small) 281.
HEIGHT: 6.5 inches
PRICE: Pair G, Singles H

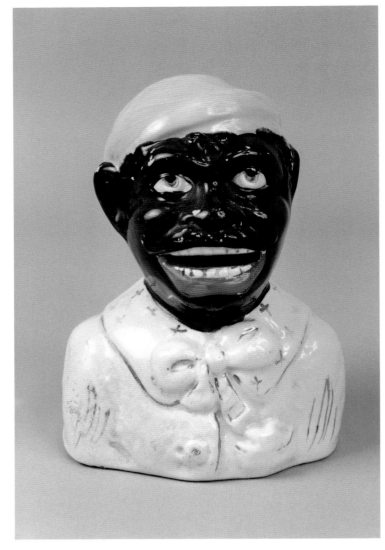

Fig. 4167
A head of a black man wearing a cloth cap, his mouth open showing his teeth.
This figure was made for use as a money box.
HEIGHT: 7 inches
PRICE: G

Fig. 4172
A standing group of two musicians, she wears a hat, blouse and long skirt with an apron, she holds and is playing a stringed instrument with both hands; he wears a tri-corn hat, jacket, shirt and knee breeches tied with a sash and is holding and playing a stringed instrument with both hands.
TITLE: MINSTRELS
HEIGHT: 10 inches
PRICE: G

Figs 4173/4174
A pair of figures of musicians seated on rockwork, he wearing a brimmed hat, shirt with tie, jacket, breeches and laced boots, a hurdy gurdy or organ is to his side, on the top of which a monkey is seated, she wearing a bodice waistcoat and long dress, holding a tambourine in her left hand.
This pair was made by the Kent Factory in about 1920; the male figure is probably the figure referred to as Organ Grinder No. 307 in the Kent list.
HEIGHT: 6.5 inches
PRICE: Pair F, Singles G

Figs. 4175/4176
(See V.S.F 1835-1875, figures. 1532/1533). A pair of standing figures of Harlequin and Columbine, both with one hand to their heads in dancing pose, he wearing a close fitting suit decorated with diamonds, she with a bodice and short skirt.
These characters are from an English pantomime. Harlequin is a mute who carried a wooden sword as a magic wand, Columbine was his mistress.
These figures were originally made in the 1860's and were later made by Kent; they are listed in the 1960 catalogue under '270 Harlequin & Columbine.'
HEIGHT: 7 inches
PRICE: Pair F, Singles G

Fig. 4177

(See V.S.F 1835-1875, figure 1148). An arbour group figure of a seated woman and a standing gypsy with a child on her back. The woman wearing a headdress, blouse and long skirt, holding out her hand to the gypsy who is standing dressed in a long cloak, bonnet and skirt with apron, the arbour is covered with a fruiting grape vine.

Two figures illustrated, the one on the left is Circa 1860; it is delicately coloured and a great deal of time was spent on the decoration, the one on the right is Circa 1920, and whilst the modelling is still good the colouring apart from flesh tones on the faces consists of just dark green splotches on the grape leaves.

It can be seen with this comparison why collectors prefer the earlier figures.

TITLE: FORTUNE TELLER
HEIGHT: 11.5 inches.
PRICE: G

Figs. 4178/4179

(See V.S.F 1835-1875, figures 2176/2177). A pair of group figures of vendors on titled bases with raised capitals, she is standing in front of a mule wearing a mop cap, blouse and dress with apron, a bowl in her right hand, her left resting on a bag of sand which is on the mule's back, he is standing in front of a mule and wearing a hat, long coat, waistcoat, shirt and trousers, his right hand holding two sticks of beesums on the saddle and two more sacks are on the ground.

Sand was used as a blotting paper and scouring agent and beesums were tied together to make brooms.

These figures were produced for a considerable period; those illustrated were made about 1900.

HEIGHT: 8.5 inches
TITLE: SAND – BEESUMS
PRICE: Pair F, Singles G

Figs. 4180/4181

A small pair of figures of standing musicians, he dressed in hat, shirt, jacket and trousers, playing a stringed instrument, she wearing a bodice and long skirt, holding a tambourine aloft.

HEIGHT: 3 inches

PRICE: Pair G Singles H

Fig. 4182

(See V.S.F 1835-1875, figure 2200A). A group of two boys, one restraining the other from taking eggs from a nest.

This figure was originally made in the 1860's by the Parr factory; this figure was made in about 1900 by their successor the Kent factory and is probably the figure referred to in the Kent list No. 338 as 'Scuffle for a nest.'

HEIGHT: 6 inches

PRICE: G

Figs. 4183/4184
A pair of standing figures of a schoolboy and girl, he wearing a cap, cloak, shirt, knee breeches and boots, holding a satchel in his right hand his left is in his pocket, she wearing a shawl, short coat and skirt, holding a slate in her left hand, her right holding her shawl at the neck.
This figure is unusual as it is decorated with both underglaze and overglaze blue; underglaze blue was hardly ever used in the decoration after 1870.
HEIGHT: 11.5 inches
PRICE: Pair E, Singles F

Fig. 4186
(See V.S.F 1835-1875 Figure 685B). A figure of a lady standing holding a spaniel, wearing a brimmed hat, jacket and long dress.
This figure is in two parts and could be used as a trinket dish. This figure was originally produced in the 1860's and was originally made as a Portrait of Princess Louise, a daughter of Queen Victoria.
This figure was made by the Kent factory and was still in production in 1960, just two years before they closed down; a line drawing of it can be seen illustrated in their catalogue for 1960 (see plate 13) where it is described as 'Crinoline No. 165.'
HEIGHT: 8 inches
PRICE: G

Figs. 4187/4188

(Ref. V.S.F 1835-1875 Figure 665/666). A pair of figures of a boy and girl seated on ponies, she seated side-saddle dressed in jacket and long dress, he seated astride wearing a jacket and trousers.

This pair of figures were very popular for very many years; they were first produced in 1863 to mark the occasion of the marriage of the Prince of Wales to Princess Alexandra of Denmark and these figures appear in our earlier book when they are titled either 'Princess of Wales' or 'Princess' and 'Prince of Wales.'

The pair illustrated were made by the Kent factory and appear in their 1960 catalogue (See Plate No. 15) as 'Prince & Princess (pair) No. 315. These figures, like the pair of Garibaldi and Napier are unusual in so far as portrait figures were never produced for very long after the event they commemorated.

HEIGHT: 8 inches
TITLE: THE PRINCESS, THE PRINCE
PRICE: Pair F, Singles G

Figs. 4189/4190

A pair of figures of a boy and girl seated holding birds with a tree stump behind, he has a nest in his right hand, wearing a jacket, waistcoat, shirt, and breeches, she holding fruit in her lap and wearing a jacket, blouse and aproned skirt.
HEIGHT: 7.75 inches
PRICE: Pair F, Singles G

Figs. 4191/4192
(See V.S.F 1835-1875, figures 2013A/2013B). A pair of figures of a girl and boy mounted, she side saddle, he astride a horse, both holding sheaves of corn aloft, other sheaves are over the saddle and on the base, she is dressed in hat and dress with a sash around her waist, he wearing a hat, shirt, waist-coat, jacket and trousers.
This pair were first made in about 1860, the pair illustrated were made in about 1900.
HEIGHT: 11 inches
TITLE: HOME, HARVEST
PRICE: Pair E, Singles F

Figs. 4193/4194
A pair of figures of a boy and girl, he seated astride, she side saddle on horses, both hold the reins and have baskets on their laps; he wears a hat, tunic and trousers, she a hat and long dress.
The long saddlecloth on this pair is similar to that on some of the late generals horses, and these figures were probably made by the Samson Smith factory.
HEIGHT: 11 inches
PRICE: Pair F, Singles G

Fig. 4195

A standing figure of a girl holding a flag aloft.

This figure is unusual, it is decorated in the manner of the Kent factory and the use of a flag with a metal pole was similar to a method used by them on a figure of Britannia. It looks as though there should be a pair for this figure and that there would have been an earlier version, but neither are known to the authors.

(Figure 4196) has been reserved for its pair should it come to light.

HEIGHT: 9.25 inches

PRICE: G

Fig. 4197

A spillvase group figure of a man and woman standing at a well, both are dressed in flowing robes, she with her right arm across her chest and the other resting on a pitcher, he wearing a turban, cloak, long coat and sandals, a rope is draped over the well which is between them.

This figure was first made in the mid 1800's and was then a representation of Christ and the woman of Sameria. (See V.S.F 1835-1875, figure 1703.) This version has been adapted, the woman is much the same but the male figure has been altered considerably, and no longer could be said to represent Christ.

HEIGHT: 12 inches

PRICE: F

Fig 4198
A figure of a standing woman, wearing a brimmed hat, bodice, jacket and long skirt, holding a pitchfork in both hands.
This figure was made by the Kent factory in about 1900. The authors have not seen an early version, and it is more than likely that this figure has a pair. (Figure 4199) has been reserved for it.
HEIGHT: 8 inches
PRICE: G

Fig 4204
A spillvase figure of a standing huntsman he wears a hat, waistcoat, long jacket and trousers with boots, holding a rifle by its barrel in his left hand and his right resting on a tree his dog sits at the base of the tree.
This figure was first made prior to 1875 and an earlier version is illustrated (See V.S.F 1835-1875, figure 1852B). There is a pair to this figure, a woman standing holding a basket over her arm with a dead rabbit in it. (Figure 4203) has been reserved for it.
HEIGHT: 11.5 inches
PRICE: G

Figs. 4205/4206
(See V.S.F 1835-1875, figures 1846/1847). A pair of figures of
equestrian hunters, wearing a highland garb of plumed hat, short
coats, kilts and sporrans, large scarves are draped over their shoulders, and a dead stag has been thrown over the horse's back.
**This pair of figures was produced for many years, firstly in the
1850's; by the end of the century they were only being made in
the white, the colouring restricted to flesh tones and overglaze
black. At some time the right hand figures headdress was
modified; on earlier figures it is a flat cap with feather.
Two pairs are illustrated – a partially coloured pair with
cinnamon horses and white bases with the remains of 'bright
gold' decoration which were made circa 1885 and a white pair
which have little decoration at all , just pink for the flesh and
black for the hair, feet and hooves and were made circa 1910.**
HEIGHT: 15 inches
PRICE: Pair F, Singles G

Fig 4207
A figure of a standing hunter dressed in highland attire, holding a rifle by its barrel, in his right hand its stock is on the ground, a dead bird lying by it, his dog is on its hind legs with its forepaws on his knee.
This figure was first produced in the 1850's (See V.S.F 1835-1875, figure 1808). This particular figure is typical of a much later production probably around 1910, little effort has been made with the decoration other than his coat and kilt have been painted a drab green, bright gold was applied but this has almost completely disappeared.
HEIGHT: 14.25 inches
PRICE: H

Fig. 4208
A figure of a huntsman standing dressed in highland garb, a rifle held by its barrel in his left hand a horn in his right, a dog standing to his left and a dead bird is on the base.
The Kent factory made this figure in about 1900. There is also illustrated an original version of the figure together with its pair that were made in the 1840's, the originals were not made by the Parr factory and therefore the moulds were probably acquired when another factory ceased production.
HEIGHT: 7.5 inches
PRICE: F

Figs. 4209/4210
A pair of equestrian figures of huntsmen facing left and right, both with deer over their horses necks, one wearing a round cap, jacket and kilt, the other with a plumed hat, jacket and kilt a scarf over his shoulder.

These figures were first produced in about 1900 and were made by the Samson Smith factory, having much in common with a number of the Boer War officer figures that were also made there.
HEIGHT: 15 inches
TITLE: HUNTSMAN
PRICE: Pair F, Singles G

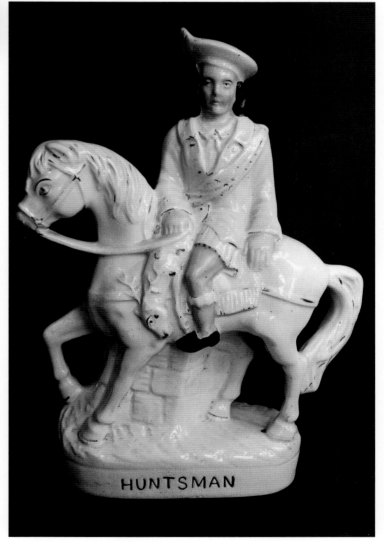

Figs. 4210

Figs. 4211/4212
A pair of equestrian figures of a man and woman, he wearing a long jacket, waistcoat, brimmed hat and trousers, she wearing a brimmed hat, and long dress, the horses are rearing up.
These figures are decorated in underglaze brown and green and were made in the late nineteenth or early twentieth century; they can be well modelled as the figures illustrated, and are said to portray 'Wild Bill Hickock and 'Annie Oakley,' although we know of no evidence to support this attribution.
HEIGHT: 12.5 inches
PRICE: Pair E, Singles F

Figs. 4213/4214
A pair of standing titled figures, she wearing a headscarf, shawl and long dress with an apron, with her hands on her hips, he wearing a top hat, shirt, tie, jacket and breeches holding pipes in both hands.
These are quite a rare pair and because of their titling quite sought after.
HEIGHT: 13.5 inches
TITLE: IRISH COLLEEN, IRISH PIPER
PRICE: Pair E, Singles F

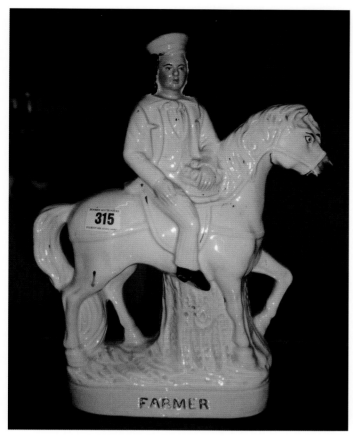

Fig. 4215
A mounted figure of a man facing right wearing a cap, jacket, waistcoat, shirt and trousers, his right hand resting on his leg, his left holding a basket of apples.
This figure is one of a pair, Figure 4216 (not illustrated) has been reserved for it, and is from the same factory as the huntsman figures. The horse in this figure is virtually identical to the horse in Figure 4209.
HEIGHT: 15 inches
TITLE: FARMER
PRICE: F

Figs 4224
A standing figure of a stout man wearing a jacket, belted trousers and a tri-corn hat, holding a mug in his right hand.
These figures were made for use as salt and peppershakers and are identical other than the number of holes in the hat, a larger than usual hole is left in the base, which is stopped with a cork.
HEIGHT: 4 inches
PRICE: H

Fig. 4251
A group figure of three clowns, standing side by side on an oval gilt lined base, all dressed appropriately, the one to the left holding a stick, the one in the middle with one arm on his shoulder and the other through the arm of the clown on the right who has both hands in his pockets.
This is a very rare figure, the one illustrated being the only one recorded. Due to its rarity and content it was eagerly sought after and the consequently high price paid for it when it was sold at auction.
HEIGHT: 14.25 inches
PRICE: C

Cottages and Houses

Cottages and houses were first produced as pastille burners early in the nineteenth century. They were made to ward off the unpleasant smells emanating from the unsanitary conditions prevalent in the towns and cities. By the late nineteenth and early twentieth century the sanitary conditions had improved and the potters consequently adapted the figures to be merely decorative objects, although some had been converted into moneyboxes. Others no longer had an aperture in the back into which a 'pastille' could be placed; most were adaptations of earlier figures although some new moulds were made, usually very simple three-piece figures.

Fig 4301
A figure of a cottage.
This appears in the 1955 Kent catalogue as 'Large Flowered' No. 194.
HEIGHT: 4.75 inches
PRICE: G

Figs 4302/4303
Two figures of cottages.
The figure on the right appears in the 1955 Kent catalogue as
'Bank cottage No. 178.'
HEIGHT: 3.5 inches & 3 inches
PRICE: H

Fig 4304 ROLL 710

Fig 4304
A figure of a cottage, multi-storeyed with two doors and a number of
windows.
HEIGHT: 4.5 inches
PRICE: H

Fig 4305
A figure of a cottage with three chimneys, four windows and steps
leading up to the door.
HEIGHT: 3.5 inches
PRICE: H

Fig 4306
A figure of a cottage with two chimneys, an eaves window, and a
double front door flanked by a window either side.
HEIGHT: 3.5 inches
PRICE: H

Fig 4307
A figure of a two-storey house with a central door flanked by
windows either side with two chimneys.
HEIGHT: 5 inches
PRICE: H

Fig 4308
A figure of a cottage with five windows and steps leading to a central
door, the roof sloping to one large chimney.
**A house could never have been built in this manner, as it would
have been impossible to have all the room's fireplaces leading
to the one chimney. Originally this figure would have been a
pastille burner with a hole at the back for the pastille, with the
smoke escaping through the chimney.**
HEIGHT: 3.5 inches
PRICE: H

Fig 4309
A figure of a two-storey house with a graduated roof; once again purely imaginary, and originally made as a pastille burner.
HEIGHT: 4.75 inches
PRICE: H

Fig 4310
A figure of a cottage with two windows, applied flowers and foliage. **The application of the flowers would suggest that this was made in the early nineteenth century, but the gilt line applied to the base is in 'bright gold' thus dating the figure to the late nineteenth, early twentieth century.**
HEIGHT: 4 inches
PRICE: H

Chapter 3: Dogs and Other Animals

Surprisingly many new dog and animal figures were produced after 1875, this in contrast to other area's of Staffordshire figures where compared to the earlier Victorian period, few new moulds were made.

Two of the main differences between pre and post 1875 figures was the use of bright gold in the decoration and the use of glass eyes in the figures; these glass eyes are similar to those used on teddy bears of the period.

Another difference was the introduction of a red/brown underglaze colouring which in some cases completely covered the figure; being underglaze it does not flake. A slate grey/black was also used to decorate the figures, in most instances these new colourings were not applied with the same skill and finesse that had been used previously.

However in the main the figures were left uncoloured with overglaze black used for eyes and whiskers and bright gold to highlight the body.

Fig. 4450
A figure of a King Charles' spaniel recumbent on a cushion with tassels at all four corners of the cushion.
The exception that proves the rule! Beautifully modelled and decorated all around. This extremely rare figure was made by the Kent pottery in about 1880. The moulds had been reused as this figure was first made in about 1830. Because the modelling is so good it is very difficult to differentiate between early and late figures and the main guide is that the colouring differs, the magenta used on the base of the figure illustrated is never seen on early figures. It is possible that a pair for this figure does exists – Figure 4449 has been reserved for it. It is however unrecorded.
HEIGHT: 7.5 inches
PRICE: A

Figs. 4451/4452
A pair of seated red and white spaniels with glass eyes, lockets and chains, their tails curl up behind.
These dogs are quite rare and unusual in so far as the red decoration is underglaze, the gilding is 'bright' gold, the method of applying a red half hoop to delineate the mouth is quite distinctive. See figures 4479/4480 for another pair produced by this factory.
HEIGHT: 9.75 inches
PRICE: Pair E, Singles F

Figs. 4453/4454
A pair of seated spaniels decorated in red with yellow enamel painted collars and lockets.
These dogs are well decorated and can be found in at least two sizes, they were made in the mid to late 1870's and the potters saved on their production costs by not gilding them at all.
HEIGHT: 5.5 & 8 inches (8 inch pair illustrated.)
PRICE: Pairs E, Singles F

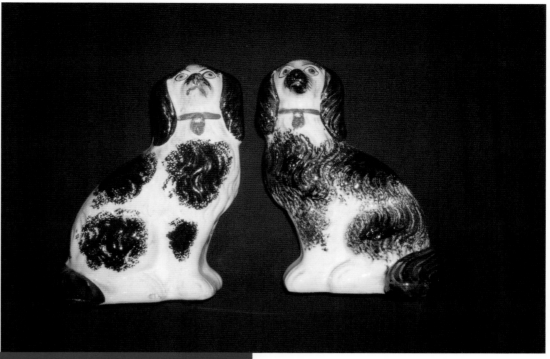

Figs. 4455/4456
A pair of seated spaniels decorated in red with bright gold collars and lockets, and a larger pair decorated in underglaze black.

This model can be found in at least four sizes and differently decorated.

The later production of spaniels showed a decline in the standard of decoration and the feathering that was common on the earlier dogs gradually disappeared and the colour was applied without the finesse previously seen, compare these figures with Figures 4453/54 and the difference in quality becomes obvious.

HEIGHT: 8.25 & 10 inches
PRICE: Pair F Singles F

Figs. 4457/4458
A pair of small-seated spaniels with yellow painted collars and lockets.

These dogs were made from simple three part moulds.

Two pairs are illustrated, identical apart from the colouring; no gilding has been applied thus economising on the cost of production.

HEIGHT: 4.5 inches
PRICE: Pair F, Singles G

Figs. 4459/4460
A pair of seated spaniels decorated in black with copper lustre chains.
These dogs are well decorated and can be dated from the copper lustre chains, they were made for a considerable period and earlier versions decorated with best gold can be found.
HEIGHT: 8.25 inches
PRICE: Pair E, Singles F

Figs. 4461/4462
A pair of white curly tailed seated spaniels with painted eyes and noses.
There is no trace at all of any gilding on this pair, either it has all been lost over the years or it never had any applied originally.
HEIGHT: 13 inches
PRICE: Pair F, Singles G

Figs. 4463/4464
A pair of seated spaniels coloured with red decoration, bright gold collars and lockets and glass eyes with tails curling in front.
Their 'pinched' faces gives these dogs an appealing surprised expression and they are well modelled and decorated.
HEIGHT: 13.5 inches
PRICE: Pair E, Singles F

Figs. 4465/4466
A pair of seated spaniels in white and gilt with painted noses.
Bright gold with which these dogs are decorated is much more prone to flaking and often, as in these figures, it has almost all disappeared; their noses have been decorated with underglaze black that in this instance has run.
HEIGHT: 13 inches
PRICE: Pair F, Singles G

Figs. 4467/4468
A pair of seated spaniels with glass eyes and gilded collars, chains and lockets.
HEIGHT: 10.5 inches
PRICE: Pair F, Singles G

Figs. 4469/4470
A pair of seated spaniels, these figures have painted eyes and
muzzles and a rather truncated curled tail.
They can be found in at least two sizes both illustrated.
HEIGHT: 12 & 14.5 inches
PRICE: Pair F, Singles G

Figs. 4471/4472
A pair of seated spaniels, once again decorated with bright gold.

Two pairs are illustrated, they are identical but over the years, probably through over enthusiastic cleaning most of the gilt decoration on one pair has been lost, this loss will now affect the price, but it is in any event very unusual to find any of these bright gold decorated spaniels with their gilding in original condition.
Also illustrated is the base of Figure 4471, this is factory marked 'SADLER BURSLEM ENGLAND.' James Sadler commenced operations in 1899 and a few figures have been found with this mark, which in turn has allowed the attribution of a number of other figures. It can also be seen that this is a slip-moulded figure as the large hole testifies.
HEIGHT: 15.5 inches
PRICE: Pair F, Singles G

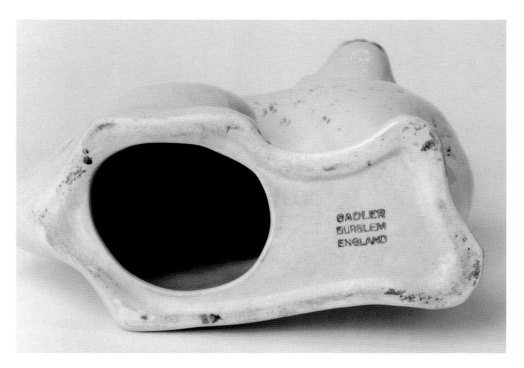

Figs. 4473/4474
A pair of seated spaniels with black painted muzzle and bright gold gilding.
The left hand side figure is illustrated. This spaniel is similar to Figure 4471 but the modelling and size is slightly different. When a figure looses its pair it is usually the left hand side figure that is broken, there are far more single right hand side figures surviving than left hand side; this has probably much to do with the fact that most people were right handed, being left handed was actively discouraged, and the left hand side figure would have been picked up with the weaker left hand. This applies to all pairs of figures, not just dogs.
HEIGHT: 12 inches
PRICE: Pair F, Singles G

Figs. 4475/4476
A pair of seated spaniels in the white with bright gold gilding, on the body, locket and chain.
The right hand side figure only is illustrated.
HEIGHT: 14 inches
PRICE: Pair F, Singles G

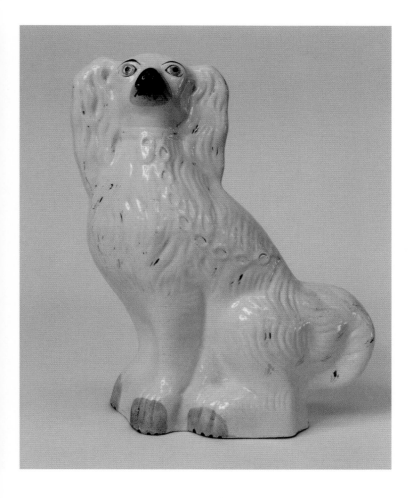

Figs. 4477/4478
A single seated spaniel in the white with bright gold gilding.
In this instance the decorator has added a small amount of grey to delineate the paws.
Also illustrated is a smaller pair of the same model of red and white spaniels with the collars and chains picked out in black. These spaniels were made in at least two sizes and can be found as illustrated decorated in a variety of colours.
HEIGHT: 11.5 & 13 inches
PRICE: Pair F, Singles G

Figs. 4479/4480
A pair of seated glass eyed spaniels, decorated with bright gold gilding, the tail curls around to the front rather than erect.
The unusual decoration to these spaniels is the red colour used to delineate the dog's mouths and is very distinctive.
These dogs can be found in at least two sizes, 10 inch version illustrated.
HEIGHT: 10 and 14.5 inches.
PRICE: Pair F, Singles G

Figs. 4481/4482
A pair of seated spaniels, tails curling upwards with painted faces and decorated with bright gold.
Left hand side figure only is illustrated.
HEIGHT: 9.75 inches
PRICE: Pair F, Singles G

Figs. 4483/4484
A pair of seated spaniels with painted faces and very curly tails decorated with bright gold.
These dogs were made in at least three sizes, all are illustrated, although unless illustrated together it is impossible to detect the size difference.
HEIGHT: 9, 9.5 and 12.75 inches
PRICE: Pair F, Singles G

Figs. 4485/4486
A pair of glass eyed seated spaniels with painted faces, lockets and chains, tails curling around in front.
HEIGHT: 10.5 inches
PRICE: Pair F, Singles G

Figs. 4487/4488
A pair of seated spaniels with lockets, collars and chains, their tails curled up behind, decorated with bright gold gilding.
These large dogs are well modelled and are similar to the underglaze brown dogs, Figures. 4505/4506.
HEIGHT: 14 inches
PRICE: Pair F, Singles G

Figs 4493/4494
A pair of seated spaniels, with collar, chain and locket, separate front legs decorated in copper lustre.
Right hand side spaniel illustrated.
These dogs were made for a considerable period; they were first made Circa 1850/60 when they were decorated with best gold and were usually either red and white or just in the white with best gold.
Manufacture of these figures continued well into the 20th century and when they are found decorated as illustrated in a hard copper lustre they date from 1920-1950.
HEIGHT: 9.75 inches
PRICE: Pair F, Singles G

Figs. 4495/4496
A pair of seated spaniels with collar and locket, separate front legs and decorated in copper lustre patches.
These dogs vary only in size and lack of chain from the previous pair.
HEIGHT: 6 inches
PRICE: Pair F, Singles G

Figs. 4501/4502

A pair of seated glass eyed spaniels.

The underglaze brown decoration is typical of late figures; it is never found on figures made before 1875 and it completely coveres the collar, locket and chain, these are probably later versions of Figures 4485/4486.

Right hand side figure illustrated.

HEIGHT: 11 inches

PRICE: Pair F, Singles G

Figs. 4503/4504

A pair of seated spaniels, the muzzle, collar, locket and chain highlighted in underglaze black the whole decorated in underglaze brown.

No gilding has been used on this pair, as both the colours used are underglaze, no flaking could have occurred.

Right hand side figure illustrated.

HEIGHT: 9 inches

PRICE: Pair F, Singles G

Figs. 4505/4506
A pair of seated spaniels with collars, lockets and chains decorated in underglaze black the body in underglaze brown.
These dogs were made in at least two sizes, both illustrated.
HEIGHT: 12 & 13.5 inches
PRICE: Pair F, Singles G

Figs. 4507/4508
A very large pair of seated spaniels with gold collars and lockets.
Two pairs illustrated one pair decorated in underglaze brown and the other white with bright gold gilding, both pairs have glass eyes.
These are large and impressive dogs that were made by the slip mould method; care was taken with the decoration, each whisker has been separately delineated.
The maker of these dogs is known to be Sadler as a pair has been found with the base of one marked 'SADLER/BURSLEM/ENGLAND.' Sadler did not start in business until 1899 consequently this would have been the earliest that they could have been made.
HEIGHT: 14 inches
PRICE: Pair F, Singles G

Figs 4509/4510

A pair of figures of seated spaniels with gilded collars, lockets and chains decorated in underglaze brown with glass eyes.

These dogs are unusual and quite rare; the shape of the ears distinguishes them from other models.

The maker of these dogs is known to be Lancaster and Sons Ltd.; the base of each bears the shield shaped stamp of this company, a mark which was used by them from Circa 1920. This company was formed in 1900 and traded until 1944, when it changed its name to Lancaster & Sandland Ltd., whilst continuing to manufacture from the Dresden Works, Hanley.

HEIGHT: 13 inches

PRICE: Pair F, Singles G

Figs. 4513/4514

A pair of spaniels seated in front of spill vases.

It is rare to find spill vase spaniels; and these figures were first made in the early 1870's, an earlier pair is illustrated in (V.S.F 1835-1875, figures. 2526/2527). They were continued in production well into the 20th century.

HEIGHT: 14 inches

PRICE: Pair E, Singles F

Figs. 4515/4516
A pair of recumbent Alsatians decorated in underglaze brown.
The omission of the base is a later innovation and is reminiscent of mid-twentieth century figures made by Sylvac and other 20th century potters.
HEIGHT: 4 inches
PRICE: Pair F, Singles G

Figs 4517/4518
A pair of standing Pugs with four separate legs, curly tails, glass eyes and collars modelled with bells.
A very appealing pair, with a lifelike expression, well modelled and quite rare.
HEIGHT: 6 inches
PRICE: Pair F, Singles G

Figs. 4519/4520
A pair of seated dogs in underglaze brown, with separate front legs and collars with bows around their necks.
These dogs are either Pugs or young mastiffs, it is difficult to determine which. They were made by the slip mould method and are very rare, the author's have only seen the pair illustrated.
HEIGHT: 7 inches
PRICE: Pair F, Singles G

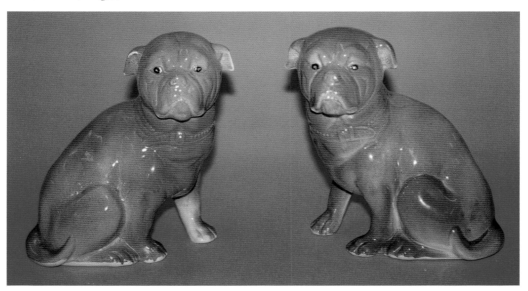

Figs. 4521/4522
A pair of figures of seated Pekinese dogs, decorated both in the white and with underglaze brown decoration.
Illustrated is a pair in the white and a single decorated with underglaze brown.
This figure was made by the slip mould method, and a vent hole the size of an old English penny is usually found in the base.
HEIGHT: 7 inches
PRICE: Pair F, Singles G

Fig. 4523
A figure of a begging dog.
This figure incorporates the new innovations of the late 1870's, glass eyes, bright gold and a red/brown decoration.
This figure is particularly well modelled and very rare, although two figures are illustrated, they are in fact identical figures with different decoration, any two will make a pair; another example of the economy of the potters, for to make a pair the tail would have to curl to the other side, making another mould necessary.
HEIGHT: 14 inches
PRICE: D

Figs. 4524/4525
A figure of a Pekinese dog seated on a cushion that has tassels at its corners.
This figure is one of a pair, Figure 4525 not illustrated.
Once again, glass eyes, bright gold and the red/brown decoration date this pair to the 1880's and later.
HEIGHT: 14 inches
PRICE: Pair C, Singles D

Figs. 4526/4527
A pair of figures of standing Pekinese dogs with bows around their necks.
Two pairs illustrated, they are more often found with the red/brown decoration, and it is very unusual to find them in black and white with a coloured base.
HEIGHT: 7.5 inches
PRICE: Pair E, Singles F

Figs 4528/4529
A pair of dogs standing four square without a base, collars around their necks.
This pair are similar to the other models produced, but the modelling of the ears are different, the figures illustrated are very early from the mould and care has been taken in their decoration, the red half hoop decorated mouth is similar to Figures 4479/4480.
HEIGHT: 10 inches
PRICE: Pair E, Singles F

Figs. 4530/4531 A pair of standing dogs with collars and lockets.
These dogs are quite well modelled, separate moulds being used for the legs and tail, this is a departure from the usual three-mould figure; a late Victorian innovation was the dispensing of the base allowing the figures to stand on their own feet.
HEIGHT: 9 inches
PRICE: Pair E, Singles F

Figs. 4532/4533
A pair of standing dogs, probably St. Bernard's.
These dogs are very well modelled and attractively decorated.
HEIGHT: 9 inches
PRICE: Pair E, Singles F

Figs. 4534/4535
A pair of standing dogs, they are similar to Figures 4530/4531 other than size and shape of head. These also have glass eyes; the potter was no doubt attempting to portray another breed.
Illustrated are a pair of black and white dogs and a single right hand side brown and white dog, these can also be found undecorated in white and gilt.
HEIGHT: 11 inches
PRICE: Pair E, Singles F

Figs. 4536/4537
A pair of dogs standing on four legs without a base.
These figures are very similar to the preceding pair, probably being just a smaller version, they do not however have collars and lockets, and the eyes are painted.
HEIGHT: 5.5 inches
PRICE: Pair F, Singles G

Figs. 4538/4539
A pair of seated dogs, probably Collies, chains around their neck and shoulders, inset glass eyes decorated partly in underglaze brown.
One glass eye is missing from the right hand side dog; when this occurs they are often replaced with modern plastic teddy bear eyes.
HEIGHT: 13 inches
PRICE: Pair E, Singles F

Figs. 4540/4541
A pair of figures of seated dogs with collar and locket, probably
Collies, by a fence.
Right hand side figure illustrated.
**These dogs are quite rare, they were first made in the early
1870's, and earlier pairs can be found (See V.S.F 1835-1875,
Figures 2795/2796). They are usually found in the white with
no colouring at all, the decoration on the base of the figure
illustrated indicates that it was made by the Kent Factory in
the early 1900's.**
HEIGHT: 6.25 inches
PRICE: Pair E Singles F

Fig. 4542
A seated figure of a Bulldog with two separate front legs and glass eyes, decorated in an underglaze
light beige and dark brown.
**A very appealing figure and very well modeled, two figures are illustrated but they are
identical, and any two will make a pair, these are very rare figures.**
HEIGHT: 7.5 inches
PRICE: F

Figs. 4544/4545
A pair of seated pugs each with a separately moulded front leg.
These figures were made by the slip mould method.
HEIGHT: 4.5 inches
PRICE: Pair F, Singles H

Figs. 4546/4547
A pair of seated Pugs on oblong shaped bases with curled tails and glass eyes.
This dog is one of a pair, left hand side figure not illustrated; Figure 4546 has been reserved for it.
HEIGHT: 11 inches
PRICE: Pair F, Singles G

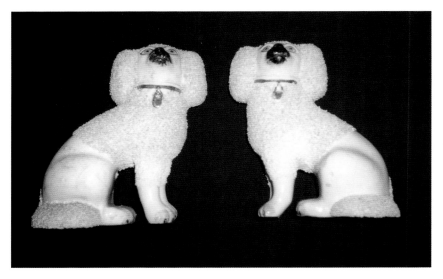

Figs 4548/4549

A pair of figures of seated Poodles, with painted eyes and muzzles, gilded collars and lockets and two separate front legs.

The decoration on these dogs gives the impression of fur, it was made by passing clay through a sieve and then applying prior to firing, they were made for a period both before and after 1875. These figures may be found decorated with either best or bright gold. They can also be found in at least three sizes and four variations (See V.S.F 1835-1875, figures 2747/47 and 2749/50).

HEIGHT: 6.5 inches
PRICE: Pair, F Singles G

Figs. 4550/4551

A pair of figures of standing Dalmatians on oval bases.

These figures were made in the Kent factory, a single left hand side figure is illustrated, as well as a pair, the single was made earlier and a comparison of the decoration on the base shows how the decoration deteriorated; the single was made in about 1880 and the colours have been applied with a 'combed' effect. By 1950 when this pair was produced combing had been abandoned and the colour applied as a coating with little skill or finesse.

HEIGHT: 6.25 inches
PRICE: Pair E, Singles F

Jackfield Spaniels

The company of Craven Dunhill & Co Ltd. were in existence from 1872 until 1951. Prior to this they were known as Hargreaves and Craven; their premises were in Jackfield, Shropshire, so technically they were not a Staffordshire potter. They made a wide range of goods including tiles; they also produced figures of dogs, which were unusual in so far as the clay used for the body was a deep red/brown in colour and they glazed them completely in underglaze black. They marked many of their figures sometimes with the full mark of CRAVEN & CO or CRAVEN DUNHILL & CO. JACKFIELD SALOP but more often they only marked the figures with the place name 'JACKFIELD.'

These underglaze black dogs proved popular and before long a number of Staffordshire potteries were also making them and figures may be found marked 'SADLER' but by transference all underglaze black dogs are now known as 'JACKFIELD' though by far the majority of them were made in Staffordshire and have a white clay body.

Fig 4552
A seated figure of a Skye terrier decorated all over in an underglaze brown. In 1858 a man named John Gray died and was buried at old Greyfriars Churchyard, being a poor man no headstone was laid; one of the mourners at his funeral was his dog 'Bobby.' The grave was closed in as usual, but the next morning he was found lying on the newly made mound. The graveyard prohibited dogs and "Bobby' was driven out, but next morning he was there again, and for a second time he was driven out. The third morning was cold and wet and the curator James Brown took pity on him and gave him food and water. From that night on, he never spent a night away from his master's grave, often in bad weather attempts were made to keep him indoors, but by dismal howls he succeeded in making it known that he wanted to sleep on his master's grave. At almost any time during the day, he could be found in or about the churchyard and stayed there for **fourteen** years until his death in 1872.
TITLE: GREYFRIARS BOBBY
HEIGHT: 7 inches
PRICE: F

Fig 4555
A seated spaniel with painted eyes, separate front leg and gilt collar and locket.
There is a pair to this figure, a mirror image, Figure 4554 has been reserved for it. Not all 'Jackfield' dogs have a body of red clay, most of those made in Staffordshire have the normal white body, and the potters used existing moulds, so these dogs can be found decorated in red and white, black and white or just gilded.
HEIGHT: 7.5 inches
PRICE: Pair F, Singles G

Figs. 4556/4557
A pair of seated spaniels with glass eyes, collars, and lockets, in underglaze black.
HEIGHT: 11.5 inches
PRICE: Pair E, Singles F

Figs. 4558/4559
A pair of seated spaniels with glass eyes and collars and chains, tails curled out behind, decorated in underglaze black.
This pair of dogs are the standard size 1 (See V.S.F 1835-1875, figures 2416/2417) with the addition of glass eyes; they were probably made by Samson Smith.
HEIGHT: 12 inches
PRICE: Pair E, Singles F

Figs. 4560/4561
A pair of seated spaniels with glass eyes, lockets and chains in underglaze black and decorated with bright gold.
This pair of dogs other than the addition of chains are the same as Figures 4505/4506, they are also marked 'SADLER' on the base.
HEIGHT: 13.25 inches
PRICE: Pair E, Singles F

Figs. 4562/4563
A pair of seated spaniels, with lockets and chains decorated in underglaze black and gilt.
This pair are very similar to Figures 4469/4470.
HEIGHT: 15 inches
PRICE: Pair E, Singles F

Figs. 4564/4565
A pair of figures of seated Pugs with a separate front leg and collars decoradet in an underglaze beige and brown. These figures were made by the slop mould method and there is a large hole in the base. **These dogs are very similar to Figs. 4544/4545 the main difference being a larger collar.**
HEIGHT: 5 Inches
PRICE: Pair F, Singles H

Figs. 4566/4567
A pair of group figures, the left hand side figure is of a dog seated outside a kennel, on the roof of which a cat is seated, a large fence is behind; the right hand side figure is of a dog chained to his kennel with his front paws on the fence on top of which the cat is seated.
An amusing pair and unusual in so far as very few new pairs of animal groups were made in the 1880's.
HEIGHT: 6.5 inches
PRICE: Pair E, Singles F

Figs. 4570/4571
A pair of seated Whippets with hares on the base.
Left hand side figure illustrated.
HEIGHT: 7 inches
PRICE: Pair E, Singles F

Figs. 4580/4581
A pair of cats with bows around their necks seated on cushions.
Two pairs illustrated identical apart from colouring.
Great care must be taken when purchasing these cats. The early pairs made in about 1850 are extremely desirable and will cost over £1000 per pair, an original pair can be found illustrated in (V.S.F 1835-1875, See figures 2869/2870). The figures illustrated were made in about 1950 at the Kent factory, a line drawing of one can be seen in their catalogue (Plate No. 14) described as 'Cat on cushion No. 67.'
HEIGHT: 7.5 inches
PRICE: Pair E, Singles F

Figs. 4582/4583
A pair of seated cats with glass eyes and bows around their necks.
A very appealing pair and typical of some of the late 19th early 20th century figures in that the figures have no base. They can be found decorated in a number of underglaze colours and also in the white; a pair of grey and a single in brown are illustrated.
HEIGHT: 12 inches
PRICE: Pair D, Singles E

Figs. 4584/4585
A pair of seated cats with separate front legs and bows around their necks.
These cats are very late and care should be taken, as they are being reproduced today.
HEIGHT: 7.5 inches
PRICE: Pair E, Singles F

Figs. 4586/4587
A pair of cats with curled tails standing on four legs, without a base, decorated in underglaze brown with painted eyes.
Very rare and very appealing for cat lovers.
HEIGHT: 8.5 inches
PRICE: Pair D, Singles E

Figs. 4588/4589

A pair of seated cats with bows around their necks in an underglaze grey/brown colouring with glass eyes, decorated with bright gold.

Two pairs are illustrated, one with brown glass eyes the other with green.

These rare figures are coloured to represent a pair of tabby cats, they are very sought after, the green-eyed cats are even rarer than the brown.

Also illustrated on the base of one of these figures is the registration mark.

From 1884 all articles of a registered design were given a number, irrespective of whether the design was in pottery, wood or metal, etc. The numbers started at 1 and by 1980 had reached 993012. The number on the base of these cats is 523391, which dates them to 1908. This is the first date that they could have been made. It is of course quite possible that they were made for a period of years after this date; they could not however have been made earlier than this.

HEIGHT: 13 inches
PRICE: Pair D, Singles E

Figs. 4590/4591
A pair of cats standing on four separate legs with tails erect, decorated in underglaze brown.
Another rare and appealing pair of cats, these were made in about 1910.
HEIGHT: 4.75 inches
PRICE: Pairs E, Singles F

Fig 4592
A figure of a seated cat with its mouth open and a bow around its neck.
There is a pair to this figure, Figure 4593 has been reserved for it.
HEIGHT: 9.25 inches
PRICE: F

Fig 4594
A figure of a seated cat with a yellow collar its tail wrapped around in front.
There is a pair to this, Figure 4595 has been reserved for it. A slip moulded figure, a very simple but very appealing model, with a smug self satisfied expression
HEIGHT: 10 inches
PRICE: Pair E, Singles F

Figs. 4610/4611
A pair of spill vase figures of cows and calves, the calves feeding from their mother.
The bright gold decoration and the palette of colours used on the base together with the blocking of the red colouring to the bodies date these figures to about 1890.
These figures were produced for a considerable period (See V.S.F 1835-1875 figures 2893/2894).
HEIGHT: 12 inches
PRICE: Pairs E, Singles F

Figs. 4612/4613
A pair of cow and calf groups, a stream runs between the cow's front legs.
These figures were produced for a considerable period, (See V.S.F 1835-1875 figures 2891/2892).
HEIGHT: 7.5 inches
PRICE: Pair E, Singles F

Figs. 4614/4615
A pair of standing figures of cows, a fence forming an oblong spill vase behind.
The Author's have not seen an earlier version of this pair although one may exist.
HEIGHT: 4.5 inches
PRICE: Pair F, Singles G

Fig. 4616
A figure of a cow with curled tail standing four square on a stand.
**This figure can be found in a number of colours and it appears
in the Kent catalogue of 1955 as Cow Cream No. 60, it could be
bought in two sizes, with and without a stand.
The figure illustrated is the 5-inch version.**
HEIGHT: 5 or 6 inches
PRICE: G

Fig. 4617
Another variant of a cow creamer.
**This one has a flatter base than Figure 4616, very often these
underglaze black figures of cows or dogs are called 'Jackfield',
this is not strictly correct; whilst Jackfield did make underglaze black figures, not all underglaze black figures were made
by Jackfield.**
Height: 5 inches
PRICE: G

Fig. 4618
Yet another cow creamer, this time in underglaze brown.
The base is slightly different from the previous two figures; this figure has retained the small cover for the hole on its back, and most often these are missing.
HEIGHT: 5.5 inches
PRICE: G

Figs 4619/4620
A matched pair of milkmaid and milkman, each standing in front of a cow, she wearing a hat, bodice, skirt with an apron and shoes, holding a bowl in her left hand, her right on the cow's back, he wearing a hat, shirt, jacket and trousers and one hand resting on the cow.
True pairs of these figures can be found where the decoration would match, where the cows are of a different colour it can always be assumed that they did not start off life together.
HEIGHT: 6.75 inches
PRICE: Pair E, Singles F

Figs. 4621/4622
A pair of spillvase figures of stags being chased by dogs.
These figures were first produced in the 1860's and an original pair can be found illustrated in (V.S.F 1835-1875, figures 2915/2916). The pair illustrated were made around 1900 and the decoration is far from good. The dating is made easy by the use of the dull green colour applied, as this was never used in the 19th century.
HEIGHT: 12 inches
PRICE: Pair F, Singles G

Fig. 4630
A figure of an Elephant standing on a gilt lined oblong base.
Two figures illustrated, any two will pair each other, very well modelled and decorated, probably made in the 1890's, they can be found in two sizes.
HEIGHT: 7.5 & 9.5 inches
PRICE: E

Fig. 4631
A figure of an Elephant seated on a round base.
Once again any two figures will pair each other, not so well modelled or decorated as the previous figure and rather more crude than naive.
HEIGHT: 6.25 inches
PRICE: F

Fig. 4632
A group figure of an elephant standing with a Mahout kneeling on its head all on an oblong base with canted corners.
This is a well modeled and rare figure the figure illustrated is delicately coloured, but examples in the white can be found, whilst this figure dates to the late 19th / early 20th century it is possible that even earlier examples could have been made.
HEIGHT: 8 inches
PRICE: D

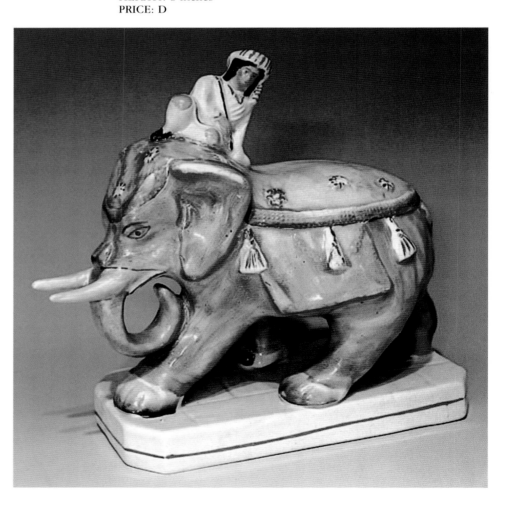

Figs. 4640/4641
A pair of figures of recumbent giraffes in front of palm trees.
These figures can be found in two sizes, a 5.5 inch pair and an 8.25 single illustrated, they were first produced in the mid 1850's and an original pair can be found illustrated in (V.S.F 1835-1875, figures 2972/2973).
The originals of the small pair are very rare and the large pair are extremely rare.
HEIGHT: 8.25 & 5.5 inches
PRICE: Pair D, Singles F

Lions

In Victorian Staffordshire prior to 1875 not many figures of lions were made and the ones that were are now very sought after and therefore expensive. Around the turn of the century one potter produced a pair in underglaze brown colouring, they must have been successful for at least four other similar pairs followed, usually with glass eyes, it is not known which pair was made first but by far the best designed pair, in the authors opinion were those made by Sadler and are illustrated in Figures 4655/4656.

Figs. 4645/4646
A pair of recumbent glass eyed lions on an oblong shaped base with underglaze brown colouring.
HEIGHT: 10 inches
PRICE: Pair E, Singles G

Figs. 4647/4648
A pair of recumbent glass eyed lions on an oblong shaped base with underglaze brown colouring.
These are different models from the preceding pair, similar but more upright.
HEIGHT: 10.5 inches
PRICE: Pair F, Singles G

Figs. 4649/4650
A pair of standing lions with glass eyes, on stepped oblong bases with one foot on a ball.
HEIGHT: 11.5 inches
PRICE: Pair E, Singles G

Figs. 4651/4652
A pair of reclining lions on an oblong bases with glass eyes.
Once again typical of late Victorian figures, these figures are coated with paint rather than decorated; the bases on this pair are better than usual, in that a degree of effort has been taken in the decoration. The colouring on the noses has given them a mournful expression, more reminiscent of bullmastiffs rather than lions.
HEIGHT: 15.5 inches (length)
PRICE: Pair E, Singles G

Figs. 4653/4654
A pair of standing lions standing four square with no base.
These are very late figures and lack all but basic decoration
HEIGHT: 6.5 inches
PRICE: Pair G, Singles H

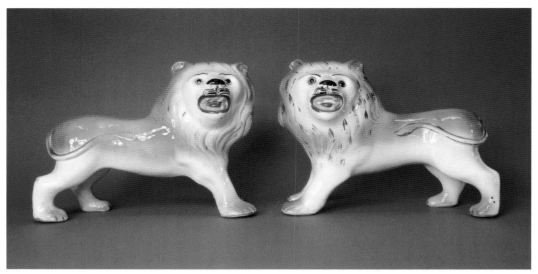

Figs. 4655/56
A pair of glass eyed roaring lions standing four square with no base.
Also illustrated is the base of a foot of Figure 4655 factory marked.
In the author's opinion these are the best modelled and designed of all the late lions, they were made in the slip mould method by Sadler and on rare occasions can be found stamped on the base of one foot in black SADLER/BURSLEM/ENGLAND.
HEIGHT: 10.5 inches
PRICE: Pair E, Singles F

Figs. 4667/4668
A pair of parrots facing left and right perched on tree stumps.
HEIGHT: 7.5 inches
PRICE: Pair E, Singles F

Figs. 4669/4670
A pair of parrots perched on tree stumps.
It is quite possible that these figures were first made prior to 1875, but the decoration, particularly on the base denotes that these were made by the Kent factory in around 1880.
HEIGHT: 8 inches
PRICE: Pairs E, Singles F

Figs. 4671/4672 A pair of Cockerels with underglaze brown decoration.
HEIGHT: 9.5 inches
TITLE: COCK O'TH' NORTH
PRICE: Pair G, Singles H

Fig. 4673
A figure of a parrot perched on a tree stump.
There is some doubt as to which factory first made this figure, shards of it were found at an excavation at the Dudson factory, and earlier versions of this figure can be found, (See V.S.F 1835-1875, figure 2834). At some time the moulds came into possession of the Kent factory and it was still being made in 1960, see plate 15 where it is described as Parrot (pair) No 102. The Kent catalogue describes a pair, but the authors have yet to see a left hand side figure.
HEIGHT: 9 inches
PRICE: F

Fig. 4674
A two part egg dish in the form of a swan, any two of these figures
will pair.
HEIGHT: 7 inches
PRICE: E

Fig 4676
A spillvase and penholder figure of a swan. These figures can be
found in pairs, the left hand side illustrated.
HEIGHT: 3.25 inches
PRICE: Pair F, Singles G

Fig. 4675
A two part cheese-keeper in the form of a swan.
**This is a very rare well-modelled and designed figure as the
neck makes a substantial handle.**
HEIGHT: 6 inches
PRICE: E

Figs. 4678/4679
A pair of standing Cockerels.
A pair of underglaze black figures and a single white figure illustrated.
These figures have become very popular, particularly with interior designers, and this has caused their price to rise. The underglaze black figures were made at the same time and by the same potters who made the Jackfield spaniels. However the cockerels fetch four to five times that of the spaniels. They were made from the early 1870's until the early 1900's (See V.S.F 1835-1875, figures 2822/2823).
The author's have also seen a pair decorated in enamel colours.
HEIGHT: 12 inches
PRICE: Pair D, Singles E

Fig. 4680
A figure of a parrot perched on a stump.
**This figure has glass eyes and was probably made early in the
20th century; it is possible that there is a pair to this figure.**
HEIGHT: 13 inches
PRICE: G

Fig. 4682
A figure of a hen sitting on a nest.
**These hen dishes were made in two parts for keeping eggs, were popular
for many years and early versions can be found. (See V.S.F 1835-1875,
figures 2828/2831.) Most are made so that any two will pair each other.**
HEIGHT: 4.5 inches
PRICE: G

Figs. 4688/4689
A pair of standing horses.
Right hand side figure only illustrated.
These figures originate from the Kent factory where they were made about 1900; a very fine pair and quite well decorated.
HEIGHT: 9 inches
PRICE: Pair E, Singles F

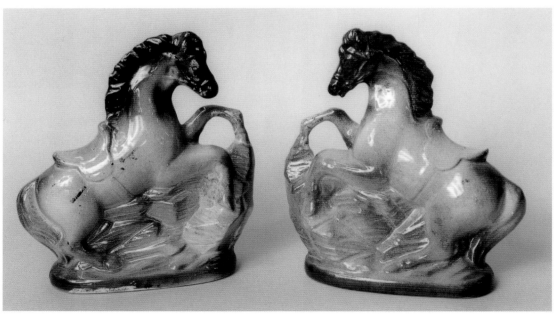

Figs. 4692/4693
A pair of rearing horses; both have reins and are saddled. They are decorated in an underglaze beige and brown.
These figures were made by the slip mould method and have large holes in the base.
HEIGHT: 8 inches
PRICE: Pair F, Singles G

Figs. 4694/4695
A pair of rearing horses on an oval graduated base. The front legs are supported by a stump.
These figures are decorated all over with an underglaze brown.
HEIGHT: 13 inches
PRICE: Pair F, Singles G

Figs. 4696/4697
A pair of spillvase figures of a sheep and a ram standing in front of a tree trunk.
**These figures were very popular and were first produced by the Parr factory in the 1860's.
(See V.S.F 1835-1875, figures 3081/3082.) They continued to be made well into the 20th
century.**
**They are listed in the Kent catalogue as Sheep and Ram and were made in two sizes, 5 and
7.5 inches; both sizes are illustrated.**
The ram is illustrated in the Kent catalogue as 'Sheep and Ram No. 107.'
HEIGHT: 5.5 inches
PRICE: Pair E, Singles G

Figs. 4701/4702
A pair of spillvase figures of squirrels eating nuts.
These figures were made around 1910, as can be seen the decoration has been coated on rather than delicately painted, earlier versions do exist but they are very rare, and would be much more expensive.
HEIGHT: 9 inches
PRICE: Pair F, Singles G

Figs. 4708/4709
A pair of figures of prancing Zebras, a pair and a single illustrated.
This pair were made earlier in about 1900. The single figure illustrated was made by the Kent factory in about 1950; a line drawing of this figure can be seen in the Kent catalogue (Plate No. 15) and was sold as Zebra (pair) No. 113.
The deterioration in the quality of the decoration can be seen; the bases on the earlier figures have the paint much more delicately applied.
HEIGHT: 4.25 inches
PRICE: Pair E, Singles F

Chapter 4: Later Reproductions

In this chapter some of the figures were first produced much earlier, and potters who in many cases were not even manufacturing in Staffordshire acquired the moulds. In other figures original moulds were not used, and a mould was taken from an original figure and then reproduced in which cases the resulting figure is usually slightly smaller than the original. Finally we have included figures that have been made to look like nineteenth century Staffordshire but they have been made to deceive and often there are no equivalent nineteenth century figures.

By 1900 the Kent factory was certainly in possession of many moulds of figures that they had bought from other potters, many, probably on the closure or failure of a factory.

The word 'reproduction' is emotive, and many would argue that as production continued, possibly without interruption, they should just be described as 'late' figures. We subscribe to this view. If the moulds passed from one factory to another whilst there would probably have been some interruption, they were still being made in Staffordshire by Staffordshire potters and there was no intent to deceive, the figures merely evolved.

These later figures are very rarely of the quality of the earlier figures. Mainly the decoration was to a much lower standard, and this is how they can be told apart. But they are and remain genuine Staffordshire figures and many are included in the preceding two chapters.

All the figures in this chapter were made after 1962 when William Kent, the last remaining potter who had been producing since Victorian times, closed down. Most were not made in Staffordshire; many were made in The Isle of Man and Taiwan. They are not factory marked nor was the country of origin stamped or impressed on them; once they have changed hands all too many are being passed off as genuine Staffordshire figures.

There is a saying that imitation is the sincerest form of flattery, if so Staffordshire figures have been continually flattered since the last figures were made in 1962. Hardly a year goes by without coming across figures that purport to be Victorian Staffordshire, but which are clearly not. We are including in this chapter many representative examples of these 'reproductions' so that the collector can be aware of what to avoid.

If a decorative figure is required there is no harm in purchasing any of these figures as such, but the price should reflect this.

Figs. 6001
A figure of a cat seated on a shaped coloured base.
This figure is a very fine REPRODUCTION. It was made not more than 20 years ago and possibly later. A great deal of time and effort was put into this figure; the base is underglaze blue and the flowers are all hand painted. There would probably be a pair to this figure, (Figure 6002 has been reserved for it).
HEIGHT: 10.5 inches

Figs. 6003/6004

(Ref. V.S.F 1835-1875, 2869/70) A pair of cats seated on a square base. Left hand side illustrated.

The figure illustrated, decorated with flowers is a reproduction and was first reproduced in the late 1970's. They can also be found decorated in a number of colours as well as being left in the white. Collectors should be very careful when purchasing these as many are being passed off as 19th century figures. The moulds were probably taken from a genuine pair and so are about a half-inch smaller than the original. The original versions now sell for above £1000 per pair, reproductions should be bought for less than £30 per pair.
HEIGHT: 7 inches

Figs. 6005/6006

A pair of seated tabby cats with kittens recumbent on oval cobalt blue bases.

These figures are fakes, they were made to deceive. To the author's knowledge, there are no equivalent nineteenth century originals. These figures were made sometime in the last ten years. They were scuffed and chipped in places where scuff and chips are unlikely to occur naturally and apart from the blue, the colouring had not been fired and was sitting on top of the glaze. If they had been original they would have cost well over £2000. They sold at auction for £400 plus the premium. Far too much for a pair of fakes, far too little had they been 'right.'
HEIGHT: 7 inches

Figs 6007/6008
A pair of cats seated on cushions with bows around their necks.
Once again in the author's opinion made to deceive. They were made in the last twenty years, the underglaze blue is quite convincing as is the patch decoration, but the painting on the faces is extremely poor.
HEIGHT: 4 inches

Fig. 6009
A figure of a seated Dalmatian.
This figure and its pair can also be found decorated as whippets. Made in the last ten years, this figure has been given an aperture to pass it off as a quill holder, the underglaze blue is particularly unconvincing
HEIGHT: 3.75 inches

Figs. 6010/6011
A pair of recumbent whippets, on blue bases.
Badly modelled, badly decorated and virtually expressionless, this particular pair have been turned out in their hundreds, should not cost more than a pound or two. The author's have seen pairs unconvincingly 'aged.'
HEIGHT: 2.5 inches

Figs. 6012/6013
A pair of seated Dalmatians on cobalt blue bases.
These are in the author's opinion the best (or worst depending on your view) reproductions to have arrived on the market. They have fooled many dealers and auction houses and during 1999/2000 have appeared with alarming frequency at auctions, fairs, and shops.
We do not know where they are being made but suspect that they are being imported from France.
To tell them from the originals is very difficult. The originals were made for a considerable period and a genuine pair can be found illustrated in V.S.F 1835-1875, figures 2682/83.
The fakes have been 'aged' by various means, not least chips and scuffing on the base where it is most unlikely to occur, but has been applied in an inconspicuous place that does not detract from the overall appearance of the fake. The gilding has also been rubbed to give the appearance of age. Most alarming of all is that the underglaze blue base is virtually the same as in pre-1860 versions.
They have been made in some quantity, and have been put in pairs into many auction houses with the clear intention to deceive.
HEIGHT: 4.75 inches

Fig 6014
A recumbent dog with its front paws crossed wearing a collar and chain, on an arched base with a hole for a quill pen.

This dog is one of a pair and their origin is unknown. They first appeared in the 1960's and they are such good reproductions that they have been passed off as genuine Victorian Staffordshire figures for many years; in fact it is still disputed by many as to whether they are 19th or 20th century figures. The modelling is very good, the gold appears to be 'best gold' the black is overglaze and as with 19th century figures has flaked, and the underglaze blue is indistinguishable from 19th century cobalt blue.

On the figure illustrated the No. '47' has been impressed in the bottom, which together with the weight (which is too light) and the feel, has confirmed the authors opinion that they are not right and that they have been made some time in the 20th century, possibly on the Continent.

This being the case would mean that Figures. 2696/2697 in V.S.F 1835-1875, are also 20th century reproductions as they were made by the same hand.
HEIGHT: 3.25 inches

Fig 6015
A figure of a hunter wearing a plumed hat, ermine edged tunic and knee breeches with boots standing holding a rifle by its barrel his dog leaping up at his side.

This figure is quite puzzling. It has been made by the slip mould method, but the clay used is a red/ brown and it has then been covered with a white slip and subsequently decorated with enamel colours, a method not used in nineteenth century Staffordshire. A lot of time and trouble has been taken to produce this figure but we do not know when or where it was made. It is possible that it was made in Shropshire by the same pottery that made Jackfield spaniels as they used a red/ brown clay.
HEIGHT: 12.25 inches

Fig. 6016
A figure of 'The Soldiers Dream,' the sleeping man dressed in full highland attire resting one elbow on a drum, a cannon is at his feet and there are two flags behind.
This figure was made in the Far East and is a copy of a genuine figure (See V.S.F 1835-1875, figure 905). It is typical of a whole range of figures now being made, it is believed in Taiwan. They have been made by the press mould method and the colouring follows the original; they have and are being made to deceive and are turning up at auctions and fairs and very often through intent or ignorance being sold as genuine. From a photograph it is difficult if not impossible to detect the difference. On close examination these forgeries are found to be heavier than the originals and the clay body darker, a fake crackerlure can also often be found to have been applied.
HEIGHT: 10.5 inches

Fig. 6017
(Original see V.S.F 1835-1875, Figure 172). A standing figure of two boxers in stylised boxing pose, a roped wall behind.
This figure has been made to deceive with intentional frit and crackerlure incorporated into the figure.
HEIGHT: 8.5 inches
TITLE: HEENAN SAYERS

Fig. 6018

A standing figure of a batsman defending his wicket.

Two figures are illustrated, one is a straight copy of a genuine figure. In the second a new head has been modelled and a beard added, the base has then been titled 'W. G. Grace.' He was the most outstanding cricketer of his time and was born in 1848 and died in 1915; no figures of him were ever made. The genuine figures of cricketers were made Circa 1850 to 1860 long before he became famous.

Its companion pair, a bowler standing by a wicket can also be found; the originals of these figures can be found illustrated in V.S.F 1835-1875, figures 3305/3306.

These figures have the dubious reputation of being the first Victorian Staffordshire figures to have been reproduced; in 1970 a number of these figures appeared on the market. Suspicion was raised as few had been seen before. The culprit was traced, but due to the apparent success it was not long before many more were made.

The figures illustrated were made to deceive, with intentional faked crackerlure incorporated into the figure. The moulds to make them were made from genuine figures, but whenever this is done the resulting fake or reproduction is marginally smaller.

HEIGHT: 10 inches

Figs. 6019/6020
A pair of Jockeys mounted facing left and right
These are a good imitation of genuine Staffordshire figures. (For illustrations of originals see V.S.F 1835-1875, figures 3314/15), but the faker has gone too far; the title has been applied in a manner never seen on genuine Victorian Staffordshire figures, and what is more, no titled figure of Fred Archer was ever produced. So if ever jockeys are found with this title they are certain to be fakes.
HEIGHT: 12 inches

Fig. 6021. A figure of a cottage with three chimneys and steps leading to the central door.
This figure was made by the slip mould method, the colours are very unconvincing as is the attempt to apply shredded clay.
HEIGHT: 4 inches

Fig 6022
A fantasy house in an oriental style.
Very well made in porcelain, nicely decorated, all in all very good quality reproduction, one of a series of such houses made by Coalport, the base is clearly stamped and there has been no effort to deceive as Coalport's factory is in Shropshire. The figure cannot really be called Staffordshire, made relatively recently, they are now collected in their own right and are antiques of the future.
HEIGHT: 4.75 inches

Fig 6023
A figure of a man and woman, she carrying a bunch of faggots on her head, he with his arm through hers holding a bottle.
This figure was originally produced in the 1850's and an original is illustrated in (V.S.F 1835-1875, figure 2179). It is NEVER found titled and is known as 'The Faggot gatherers' and is 12 inches tall. This 'copy' is 11.5 inches and has been given a spurious title in black capitals 'HIGHLANDER.' As neither of the figures are dressed in highland attire, the title is not only wrong but clearly made to deceive the unwary.
This and the next six figures all have been made quite recently, it is believed in the Far East. None are factory marked and the authors have seen these and many others of their ilk, either through intent or ignorance being passed off as genuine Victorian Staffordshire figures, as new ornaments not more than £5 should ever be paid for them.
HEIGHT: 11.5 inches

Fig 6024
A figure of 'The Victory.'
A copy, and a very bad one at that, of one of the most sought after and therefore most expensive Victorian Staffordshire figures. The original is illustrated in V.S.F 1835-1875, figure 801 and is 14.25 inches high and was only ever made in that size, this appalling copy is 8 inches high.
HEIGHT: 8 inches

Fig 6025
A Figure of Nelson and the Victory.
Another bad copy of a genuine figure see (V.S.F 1835-1875, figure 229). The original was made in two sizes 5.5 and 3.75 and is never titled; this copy has his hat wrong and is titled in a style and script never seen on genuine figures.
HEIGHT: 6 inches

Fig 6026.
A standing figure of Napoleon on a square base.
This is a very bad copy of the tallest recorded Victorian Staffordshire figure (See V.S.F 1835-1875, figure 42). The original is 24 inches high and less than five are known to exist all of which are titled in gilt script, not in raised capitals.
HEIGHT: 9 inches

Fig 6027
A standing figure of Beaconsfield.
The original version (See V.S.F 1835-1875, figure 4056) was made in two sizes 14.5, 16.5 inches; no original 5 inch version has been recorded.
HEIGHT: 5 inches
ROLL Photo only

Fig. 6028
A seated figure of Will Watch.
The original version (See V.S.F. Figure 1222) for an example of the original which is 13 inches high, the titling on this copy is particularly badly executed and there has also been an attempt at faking the crackerlure.
HEIGHT: 10 inches

Fig 6029
A group figure of a boy and girl standing, titled 'TENNIS – CRICKET.'
Once again a copy of a genuine figure but the original has never been found titled.
HEIGHT: 7 inches

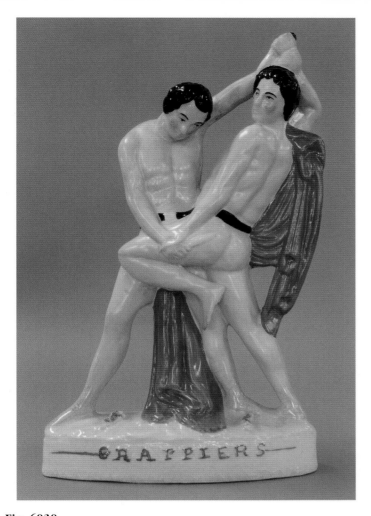

Fig. 6030
A group figure of 'The Grapplers.'
For an illustration of an original (See V.S.F 1835-1875, figure 3301). This figure is by far the best copy of a Victorian figure that we have seen, and from the photograph it is almost impossible to tell from an original; indeed it is so good that it will in time deceive many. We do not know where they are being made. The figure illustrated was purchased via the internet for £20, and was sold as a reproduction; however if reproductions of this quality are made of other figures, it will need an expert to distinguish them from originals.
HEIGHT: 11.5 inches

Fig. 6032
A group figure of a cat with three kittens all on an oblong base.
Badly modeled and even worse decorated, reminiscent of The German fairings made before the Second World War and then sold for pennies. A very bad attempt to reproduce an early Victorian figure.
HEIGHT: 3 inches

Fig. 6031
A figure of a spaniel's head, this figure was made to serve as a tobacco jar, and is a copy of an earlier figure, see V.S.F. 1835-1875 figure 2585.
The original of this figure has another laying spaniel on the lid, the reproduction has reduced this spaniel to a knob.
HEIGHT: 6 inches

Index

US $49.95

9780764317996   54995

ISBN: 0-7643-1799-7